PIPPA'S PROGRESS

PIPPA'S PROGRESS

A Pilgrim's Journey to Heaven

SIMON PARKE

DARTON·LONGMAN+TODD

First published in 2012 by
Darton, Longman and Todd Ltd
1 Spencer Court
140 – 142 Wandsworth High Street
London SW18 4JJ

ISBN: 978-0-23252954-8

A catalogue record for this book is available from the British Library.

Designed and typeset by Judy Linard
Printed and bound in Great Britain by Bell & Bain, Glasgow

To my lost friend who
taught me to write.

The candle always burns.

'To become fully yourself is a terrible risk. It would commit you to God knows what and lead you God knows where.'

H. A. Williams

Every book is a partnership, the work of a community and this book is no different. So my particular thanks to Martin Wroe for his encouragement in the pub to run with the idea when I wasn't sure; to Angela Reith for that difficult book title; to Clive Williams, Angela Reith, Shellie Wright and David Moloney for reading and commenting on a work in progress. (I almost always followed your advice.) Thanks also to Harry Parke for the marvellous cover and illustrations; to Shellie Wright for a significant contribution to one of the scenes and to my gracious editor David Moloney, managing editor Helen Porter, designer Judy Linard and all at DLT for their skill, labour and wonderful sense of adventure. Finally, I must thank the real 'Pippa', on whose birthday, May 17th, I send off the final manuscript.

Let it be.

Contents

Introduction

Pippa's Progress is an allegory, a story in which everything means something. Perhaps, for instance, you face a hard choice at the moment. If your life were an allegory, we might say you're walking through the Valley of Decision. It would be a metaphor for your state, a way of understanding it. This valley has a particular meaning.

As a story form, allegory is a triumph of human development. It arose in ancient times amid growing psychological and spiritual sensitivity, a developing awareness of the divided will in every human soul. How could such inner struggles and joys be spoken of? One way was to use metaphors, to say 'It's like this'. And one of the best metaphors is the idea of the journey.

Of course, it's very twenty-first century to be 'on a journey'. The phrase is the calling card of every wannabe celebrity. But John Bunyan was there before them in the seventeenth century when he wrote *Pilgrim's Progress*, and three centuries later C. S. Lewis followed him with *Pilgrim's Regress*. (Remarkably, Bunyan's work, written in a prison, went on to become the seventh-best-selling book of all time.)

Writing in another era, Lewis' characters and settings differed from Bunyan's and *Pippa's Progress* is different again. Times change. But all three stories share the idea of journey; of a seeker facing the joys and challenges of pursuing truth in the contemporary world. It's exciting stuff.

So *Pippa's Progress* is an adventure story. All human emotion is here, awfulness and beauty and the consequences played out. But it's also a satire because there's much nonsense in the world dressed as truth; so sometimes on the path we make a virtue of ridicule. Readers also say it's a bit scary at times, a bit sad at times and sometimes very funny. Perhaps most of all, though, it's a love story.

You'll relate and react variously along the way. Pippa's story may not be yours but her search is. Journey on with her through the light and the dark and you'll make your own progress.

The first stage

Neither in life nor death do we know what's round the corner. Take Pippa, now terrified and tumbling downwards through the air.

On a morning like any other morning, she trips on her dressing gown at the top of the stairs. It's easy to do but hard to recover and she's falling backwards into screaming oblivion when the visitor catches her in strong arms.

'Are you OK?' he asks.

'It's nothing,' gasps Pippa, before yelling 'Agghh!' as pain strikes.

'Keep still and we'll get you to a comfortable place,' says the man. 'Just relax, you're quite safe.'

And in truth Pippa does feel safe.

'So who are you?' she asks, as step by step, she's carried down the stairs.

'Who do you say that I am?' asks the visitor.

'Who is anybody?' says Pippa.

'Good question.'

'It is, isn't it? And to be honest, one I'm asking more and more often these days.'

'Really?'

'Oh yes. I mean, some people say we're just a skin full of chemicals.'

'Interesting.'

Pippa's now thinking how strange life is. The man's identity is a mystery, yet here they are engaged in deep metaphysical discussion before reaching the bottom step.

'I could even offer the question back,' says the stranger, 'and ask who are you?'

'Who am I?' splutters Pippa as she's borne through the hallway.

A worm has turned; enough is suddenly enough.

'I'm the person who lives here,' she says, 'and I want to know what you're doing on my property!'

Certain things were becoming clear. It was good this man had saved her life but not good that he was trespassing. She had questions that needed answers.

'My name's Will Good,' he said, 'and I help people move.'

'Oh, I see,' replied Pippa, not seeing at all.

'You do want to move, don't you?'

'Well, I – '

'I was told you rang.'

'I don't remember ringing anyone,' said Pippa. 'But it's true, I am a little tired of my present address. I've been here a long time, too long perhaps.'

'So you must set off immediately.'

At this point Pippa became aware of her altered surroundings. It was still her front room but not as she'd left it.

'Wait a minute,' she exclaimed. 'Where's all my furniture gone?'

The visitor had laid her on the sofa, but apart from that the room was entirely bare. It was as though removal men had entered the property and thoroughly cleared the place. And as it turned out, they had.

'We emptied the place while you slept,' he explained.

'A bit presumptuous.'

'In preparation for your departure. We didn't want to delay you. We've sent the furniture on.'

'But perhaps I'm in no great hurry to leave!' she remonstrated.

'Really? I heard you were unhappy.'

Pippa tested out the damaged foot with pleasing results. The injury was not serious.

'Possibly,' she admitted.

'I heard you felt weighed down by things, trapped in a mechanical existence, your course set in the dull grooves of habitual reaction. A life lived more from habit than joy; low-grade angst with sporadic regret and dissatisfied longing.'

Those wouldn't quite have been Pippa's words but they did ring bells.

'Sure,' she said hesitantly. 'But that doesn't mean I have to leave right now.'

Will Good was looking out the window.

'Sounds like a good reason to me,' he said, 'but you always were a professor of procrastination and excuse.'

There was an awkward pause. In Pippa's world, it was impolite for intruders to indulge in personal observations, however true they might be.

But on looking around the empty space, Pippa felt a strange calm. She was trying to be offended by the visitor but failing.

'I suppose it is time to be going,' she said.

Will was silent.

'I mean, you do reach a time in life when you have to go,' continued Pippa.

Still no response.

'Perhaps we only ever leave when we're bored of our unhappiness,' she said, aware how bored she was with her own. 'You know, when we realise it has nothing new to say.'

And in that moment, somewhere and somehow, the decision was made and the universe changed. Pippa was leaving home and now needed information.

'You must tell me the route,' she said, striking an adventurer's pose of hands on hips and enigmatic gaze into mid-distance.

Will Good smiled.

'Did you hear what I said?' asked Pippa.

'About needing a route? Yes, but I wouldn't worry about that.'

'I worry about it very much!' she said, enigmatic gaze abandoned. 'I'll need a route, I think!'

'On the journey to heaven – '

'I beg your pardon?'

'That's what you said in your phone call.'

'The call I don't remember making.'

'You spoke of journeying to heaven.'

'Well, I've always wished for heaven, obviously. But then doesn't everyone?'

'They do. But here's the difference: not everyone sets out on the journey. And you said you would.'

Pippa pondered awhile and when Will left the room for a moment, she got out her diary and started to scribble:

This person is slightly unnerving me. Professor of procrastination and excuse? That's rude, however you look at it. I suppose it's true that even in these secular times many people do wonder about heaven without doing a great deal about it. And it's possible I have been one of those until now. Not that I'll be telling him that. Survival rule No. 1: Never admit weakness, Pippa.

At this point, Will Good returned.

'Do you know what?' said Pippa, ready for a fight back.

'Please tell me.'

'Perhaps more people would set out on the journey to heaven if they knew the way,' she said.

'Do you think so?'

'Absolutely,' she declared, like a world authority on the subject. 'No one knows the way and that's why they don't make much progress!'

'Is that why you've never done anything about it?'

'Who says I haven't?'

Another uncomfortable pause.

'Believe me, the way to heaven is never a problem,' said Will, gathering his things to go.

'How so?'

'Simple. When you set out on the journey, the way finds you.'

'Oh it does, does it?'

'It is one of the stranger truths, I grant you, but, yes, creation conspires to help you.'

'How very convenient!' said Pippa sensing woo-woo in the air. 'How very, very convenient!'

'Well, it's not always convenient,' said Will, and as he spoke, Pippa noticed the scars in his hands. 'Indeed sometimes it's rather inconvenient. But it's clear enough when it comes. You just have to trust the path and keep on walking.'

And this is what Pippa did, though the 'trust' part came and went and she did occasionally stumble a little, as you do on adventures.

She finally left home later in the day after Will Good had gone.

'I must fly,' he'd said, 'but I wish you all the best on your travels, Pilgrim.'

'Sorry?'

'Pilgrim, it's your name.'

'Pilgrim? What sort of a name is that?'

'The name you had before you had a name.'

'I see,' said Pippa.

She liked her old name, to be honest. It was who she was, so the new name was a little unsettling.

'And remember,' added Will, 'heaven is for the brave and that's definitely you.'

'Me?'

'Most certainly.'

'Well, if you say so,' said Pippa, 'though I've never really thought of myself as brave.'

'Then start now.'

'I will. Yes, I will! And thank you for catching me when I fell.'

'My pleasure. I could have sent angels but I thought "Why not do it myself"?'

'Angels?'

'I'm joking.'

'Ah!'

Pippa sat alone for a while with some tea and toast spread thick with honey. She looked around at the empty space that had once been her home. Much had happened here down the years and not all of it beautiful; but in a strange way she wouldn't change anything for it had brought her to now, to this moment when all seemed possible.

'Dear Diary,' she wrote, '*I am happy to be myself at this moment. Everything's quite perfect. And everything's possible.*'

She remembered her final conversation with Will Good.

'Along the way, Pilgrim, allow for the rhythms of the seasons and the changing moods of the sky.'

'Life is change!' she'd said with nervous excitement.

'Yes it is and life is listening to where you are,' said Will. 'On your journey, every hill has a name, every path a purpose, every clearing a meaning.'

This all sounded very intriguing.

'Does the path itself have a name?' she asked.

'It's just the journey really. But I'm aware the locals give it a name.'

Will suddenly looked sad.

'What is it?' asked Pippa.

'They call it The Path of Yortether.'

'Why's that?'

'Because when you get to the end of Yortether, then you start to see.'

'Well, that sounds very encouraging.'

'It does? Then go well, Pilgrim.'

'Thank you, Will, I shall. And you too, you too! I don't suppose we'll meet again ...'

But Will Good was gone.

Pippa washed her cup and plate, left them down-turned on the draining board and turned off all appliances except the fridge. You never turn off the fridge, even if you're going to India for six weeks.

She walked from empty room to empty room, said 'thank you' in each, stood in the hallway for a moment and then, with a deep breath, pulled open the front door, walked through and closed it behind her. This was it. No turning back, not even to check the iron, a habit that sometimes delayed her arrival at work. She'd once returned to check it seven times. Not today.

And brave Pilgrim was just starting down the path to heaven when her neighbour called out over the hedge. His name was Consultant – or Con for short. He earned his living by hiring himself out expensively to tell others to do things he never did himself. He spoke of blue-sky thinking, though he seemed to live under a perpetual cloud.

'Where are you going?' asked Con.

'I'm starting out on my journey to heaven,' said Pilgrim.

'In which case I have some good news for you.'

'What sort of good news?'

'I can save you that journey.'

'Really?'

'Oh yes, trust moi! I mean, who wants a journey when you could just attend a conference?'

'A conference?'

'Comfortable chairs, comfortable learning.'

'A good slogan.'

'I thought so. Discovery in a relaxed but enquiring environment tailored to your individual needs.'

'You speak like a brochure.'

'And here's mine. I hope you like it.'

He slipped a glossy booklet into Pilgrim's hands. The chairs did look comfortable.

'It does sound a lot easier,' she agreed.

'A whole lot easier. I put the Cor! into corporate hospitality.'

'No mean feat.'

'And it just so happens that my next conference is on the subject of heaven.'

'That's exciting. What's it called?'

'Does heaven above make for hell below?' Clever, eh?'

'You're a very clever Con.'

'And that's the sort of know-how, the sort of expertise you're buying into.'

'And what actually is your expertise?' asked Pilgrim hopefully. She needed all the help she could get in the business of heaven.

'A great deal as it happens. For £1000 – '

'£1000?'

'The coffee's extra, obviously.'

'Obviously.'

'I offer a general overview of the subject, debates past and present, the history of heaven, that sort of thing, while putting it in some sort of socio-dynamic perspective.'

'OK.'

Pilgrim was wondering why Con wore dark glasses when it wasn't sunny, but he remained in full flow.

'That's then followed by a targets-based hands-on out-of-the-box look at your personal or work goals and possible outcomes in terms of short-term and medium-to-long-term objectives.'

Pilgrim was hearing only noise.

'I'm sorry,' she said, 'but I don't know what you're talking about.'

On reflection, she often felt this when talking with Con.

'It's a solutions-based scenario,' he explained. 'Where are we now? Where have we come from? Where do we want to be?'

'I want to be on my way,' said Pilgrim.

'And for a small fee,' said Con, ignoring her, 'my *The Heaven Myth and You* DVD will be thrown in free of charge.'

'Free of charge for a small fee? How could I say no?'

'But most important of all – and this is the clincher, Pippa – it'll save you all that journeying business which can be unsettling.'

'I'm sure you're right.'

'So I assume I can count you in?'

Pilgrim stood in her garden and watched a robin alight on the fence. Could Con count her in?

'No, you can count me out,' said Pilgrim.

'Why so?'

'I feel something good inside me is being stifled.'

'That's just my point, Pippa.'

'And you're stifling it.'

'Me?'

Shocked silence.

Where to begin with the Con man? Eternity was too short.

'Heaven's a journey not an idea,' said Pilgrim. 'You're an expert in the theory of heaven but not the experience. I want the experience, my friend.'

Con stood open mouthed.

'You're making a serious mistake, Pippa.'

'Oh, and one more thing,' she said.

'What's that?'

'My name's Pilgrim.'

Just then, a butterfly appeared from the flowers, a flapping miracle of orange and blue. It danced past Pilgrim, fluttering its merry way towards the gate. Pilgrim watched it and decided to follow.

'Reduced rates and coffee included!' pleaded Consultant. 'And a lifetime subscription to *Conference Weekly*!'

'Shoot me if I ever read that,' said Pilgrim under her breath.

But just as one voice faded and Pilgrim sensed heaven in the air, another voice pierced the quiet, pressing for Pilgrim's attention.

'Hi, I'm Mags,' it said.

Mags must have been a friend of Con as she'd been sun-bathing in his garden.

'Hello, Mags,' said Pilgrim reluctantly. She was eager to be on her way.

'My friends call me "Glossy".'

'"Glossy" Mags?'

'At your service, because I couldn't help but hear you talking of heaven and that is so me!'

'How exactly?'

'I offer body heaven, darling.'

Pilgrim wasn't sure about the 'darling'.

'How does that work?'

'Tell me, luscious: what do most women want?'

'Well – '

'I'll tell you what we want, what we really really want! We want to look young and we want to look thin! Simple as.'

'I suppose.'

'Every real woman is displeased with their body, babe. End of!'

'End of what?'

'It's why at any given moment, 50 per cent of us are on a diet. Go figure!'

Pilgrim found Glossy's face slightly unnerving.

'Why are you looking at me in that odd way?' asked Pilgrim.

'I'm looking at you in a young way, honey,' she replied. 'Nip, tuck and all that.'

Glossy tried to smile but struggled as most of her face was behind her ears, leaving only drum-tight skin around her nose (recently chiselled) and her eyes (long-term desperate.)

'I'm young again!' she exclaimed.

'You look slightly ill to me,' said Pilgrim.

'Get down off your high horse, you snooty bitch!'

Pilgrim's eyebrows raised a little.

'Only joking!' said Glossy.

'I don't see anyone laughing.'

Pilgrim made a point of looking around.

'But surely you compare your body with those around you?' continued Mags. 'Everyone does!'

'I do sometimes,' admitted Pilgrim.

'There!'

'And to be honest, it doesn't usually improve my mood.'

'Precisely. So have you considered the tapeworm diet?'

'Real tapeworms?'

'Is that a problem?'

'Sort of.'

'But they eat everything!'

'You're not selling them to me.'

'So why not try the Master Cleanse diet?'

'What's that?'

'Lemon water, cayenne pepper – '

'Any others?'

'I've got it. The apple cider vinegar diet. After that, your taste buds are completely – '

'Good bye, Glossy.'

Pilgrim suddenly felt happy about her body in a way she'd never felt happy before and, with the butterfly leading, she set off to follow with fresh vigour. But Glossy Mags pressed on.

'Look, if it's a new bum you want or hugely inflated pair of – '

'I'm happy as I am!' Pilgrim called back.

The unrealistic ideals of Glossy Mags had lost their power, but she wouldn't give up. The last words Pilgrim heard were these: 'Remember to drink 14 litres of water a day, fatty! And if you change your mind about the tapeworms – '

At the end of the path, Pilgrim came to the wicket gate. She opened it, walked through and closed it behind her. It went 'click' as it always did, only this time it was final. Beyond the gate, she looked up into the sky, noted a bird hovering – a hawk perhaps? – breathed in trust, looked to the horizon and started walking because, having escaped the neighbours, that's what you do if you want to get to heaven.

The second stage

On the journey to heaven, the path does come and find you. But beware: this doesn't mean you don't meet tigers along the way. I mention this because even now there's a large tiger watching Pilgrim as she crosses a piece of wasteland. Perhaps this ground had once been cared for; there were rusting signs and old line markings on the tarmac. But these days it was neither one thing nor the other, overgrown with winding weed and not quite wanted by anyone.

'I know the feeling,' thought Pilgrim.

Would it have helped to know what lay ahead as she closed the gate behind her? Should Will Good have warned her of tigers when they talked? He'd told Pilgrim to trust the path and keep on walking but that's easier said than done when killer cats are about. Pilgrim was doing her best to keep her spirits up.

'You can't go back and if you try you fail,' she repeated to her self. 'So you face what is, even if it's a prowling tiger!'

But action was necessary. As her aunt often observed, 'Fine words butter no parsnips', and Pilgrim now began to walk away from the beast.

'Friend or foe?' she called out playfully but the tiger just stared, allowing Pilgrim to move ahead.

The animal was wonderfully coloured, sleek and graced with easy power. Pilgrim decided she'd be a very good friend but a terrible foe and the latter was looking more likely. The tiger was stalking her but keeping thirty yards between them.

It wasn't a comfortable thirty yards. Between humans, personal space is reckoned at eighteen inches but between human and tiger, thirty yards is unsociably close and Pilgrim's stroll soon became a jog. Rising to the challenge, the tiger joined in the game, padding forward with a spring in its sharp-clawed paws. And so it was the gentle chase started.

Pilgrim knew one thing for certain: 'honours even' was not a possible outcome. Someone would leave disappointed or dead and Pippa didn't want to die. Sweat broke out down her back and she began to run faster.

'Thank God for last week's visit to the gym and the occasional yoga!' she thought.

But despite the yoga, the tiger was closing.

Then quite suddenly the creature stopped and Pilgrim followed suit; she'd no choice, finding herself at the edge of a cliff. Her escape route had come to an abrupt end and only continued a hundred yards below. No wonder the tiger had been in no particular hurry. It wasn't as if Pilgrim was going anywhere. 'This is not a good place for a cliff,' thought Pilgrim, pausing to consider her options. Behind her was a hungry tiger; in front of her, a sheer drop.

'Choices, choices.'

If she jumped, she wouldn't get eaten which was good; but she would get smashed to pieces on the rocks. If she didn't jump, she wouldn't get smashed on the rocks, which was good, but she would get eaten. So both options had their pros and cons but neither offered Pilgrim her desire to live and breathe one more tomorrow.

The tiger moved forward, impatient for the kill, and suddenly Pilgrim was looking at the vine. There was a vine which ran down the cliff face, strong, thick and rooted in the scrub by her feet.

'If God gives you lemons you make lemonade,' as her aunt also observed, so taking hold of the vine, she swung herself over the side of the precipice.

It was hard to exchange solid land for thin air but the approaching monster eased the decision. Pilgrim was gripping the vine and trusting its strength. She had no choice as the large cat stood at the cliff edge snarling displeasure with his victim just five feet from his salivating mouth and terrifying teeth. Pilgrim clung on tight as her feet searched desperately for crack and crevice in the rock.

Her arms ached but she was still in the game which is the first requirement when chased by tigers.

'Let's look at the positives,' she said to herself. 'Here I am, inching away from the beast towards safety. There's a long way to go but perhaps I can make it?'

It's the golden rule of climbing that you never look down. It's not encouraging to see the clean air between you and the ground below or to know how far your soft body has to fall and how sharp the rocks are that await you. But when Pilgrim could resist no longer and stole a glance downwards, it was even worse than that. Not only was there a big drop beneath her; but at the bottom of the big drop she could see lurking there another tiger.

Ye gods! This was not what Pilgrim had signed up for. She was hoping for heaven but experiencing hell. There was now a tiger above her and a tiger below her and both creatures knew Pilgrim was their best chance of a meal for a hundred miles around.

'I don't want to die,' said Pilgrim tearfully, as she struggled to keep hold of the vine. Why had she not spent more time on the ropes in PE? Truly, this was the most hopeless situation she'd ever been in and the worst thing about hopeless situations is that they're hopeless; there seems absolutely no way out.

And then matters got worse.

The only thing keeping Pilgrim safe was the vine.

'The vine is central to everything,' thought Pilgrim sweatily, and it was true.

This strong tentacle of hope had helped her inch clear of the tiger above and was keeping her safe from the tiger below. Her feet were finding brief footholds but they were temporary and crumbling and none gave refuge for her pumping heart and burning hands. It was the vine that was her strong hope, the golden thread by which she might be saved.

Yet now this saving vine was being eaten by a rat. Would you believe it? Where the rat had appeared from, hell only knew, perhaps from hell itself. They say you're never more than twenty-five feet from these vermin and that was certainly true now, for here it was, somehow steady on the rock face and nibbling and gnawing away; a rat with a mission and destroying everything that offered Pilgrim safety.

When someone threatens, it's hard not to hate, and how Pilgrim hated the rat! She imagined a huge trap springing down and crushing its neck; but such fantasies did nothing to stop the nibble and gnaw. With the vine weakening, it was only a matter of time before she fell to earth with back-breaking impact to face death by mauling. What was all that nonsense about looking on the bright side of life? There was no bright side here.

Pilgrim did her best. She shook the vine to dislodge the rat. She twisted the cord to make the vermin lose its footing, but to no avail and when finally the end came, it came fast. The vine tore and Pilgrim was falling. In a way, it was a relief; at least she could give up hope now.

'Goodbye hope!' she screamed. 'Land of hope then gory!'

People talk of hope as a good thing but when it sneers in your face, there's nothing good there at all. Better by far to say goodbye to hope and, having done so, Pilgrim was almost relaxed as she hit the ground.

What a view! Winded but conscious, Pilgrim looked directly into the ferocious face of the beast and if not a joy to behold, it proved a memorable sighting of the tiger's incisors.

'It's like a really good nature programme,' thought Pippa, 'only sadly, I'm in it.'

The sheer majesty of the creature was remarkable; a cavernous roar like honey and diamonds and strong haunches preparing to strike. Pilgrim closed her eyes and waited; she waited for the slamming jaw to come down on her scrawny neck.

What had her life ever really meant?

And then silence.

Something had changed; something formerly present was now absent. Pilgrim lay still, paralysed to everything but execution. Yet she was safe. She knew she was safe even though she couldn't open her eyes. And what she saw when she did open them was the tiger slinking away into the bush. It moved in a hurried and irritable manner but for Pilgrim the terror was over. She had another day to live, another moment to breathe, another tomorrow to contemplate.

Her diary entry was brief but happy:

I'm alive!

For a while she lazed in the dry grass and thistle, utterly content. Then she danced a victory salsa around a tree before lying down again. A butterfly emerged from a dark corner and in mad flight almost took her nose off before flying away.

'See you later, blue and orange butterfly!' Pilgrim shouted cheerily before a question came into her mind: how had it all happened?

'Here I am safe and sound,' she thought, 'when really I ought to be dead. Instead of being mauled by a tiger I'm chatting to butterflies. How did that happen?'

She knew she was alive but had no idea how or why it was so.

And then suddenly she was tense again with fear. There was disturbance in the undergrowth which Pilgrim could hear but not see. Was it a snake? It could be a snake; arid scrubland like this was full of them. What a bleak thought: had she been saved from the tiger only to be killed by a snake? In the absence of sight, imagination does sometimes party.

There was more movement and a squeaking noise. Pilgrim rolled away frightened, aware of something close by, small but unrevealed. It was the worst sort of enemy, an enemy she couldn't see, and then she did. Sitting on a rock, its paws in the air like a beggar, was the rat who'd so nearly caused her demise. Pilgrim pondered the most painful death she could inflict on the creature.

Yet as she looked more closely, something strange happened: the rat began to squeak to her or perhaps speak to her? Pilgrim was beginning to hear words and if they weren't coming from the rat where else were they coming from?

'You owe me,' said the vermin.

Pilgrim was taken aback but didn't feel like conversing with an animal.

'I'm sorry but I don't talk to animals,' she said, clarifying things at the outset.

The rat was silent and Pilgrim, feeling she'd been a little blunt, expanded a little. 'It's not personal.'

'Really?' said the rat.

'Well, it is personal but it's also true that I don't do it. I'm on my way to heaven not la-la land, so conversations with animals are not going to happen; not in a million years.'

'We have nothing to offer you?' said the vermin. 'Then fair enough, I suppose.'

There was an awkward pause which again Pilgrim felt honour-bound to fill.

'I'm glad you see it in that light,' she said. 'As I say, it's nothing personal. I'm human, you're an animal and I just don't want to know you.'

'Likewise,' said the vermin.

'I beg your pardon?'

'I have no great wish to know you either,' said the vermin. 'I wouldn't have come unless asked.'

'Well I didn't ask you.'

'Who said you did? But you still owe me.'

Pilgrim could hardly believe her ears.

'Me owe you? If it wasn't for you, I'd be safe up my vine!'

The rat smiled the smile of one who's just heard something ridiculous.

'Safe up your vine? That's an interesting take on the matter. Have you always been blind or is it a recent condition?'

'That was a good vine and you ruined it.'

'So, as you hung between two tigers, half way down a cliff, what exactly was your plan of salvation?'

Pilgrim had no desire to be caught up in a meaningless debate with an animal and opted for dignified silence. The other reason being the vermin was right. Pilgrim had had no plan.

'There was only one way to save you,' continued the rat. 'Get you to the ground and then deal with the tiger, which, fortunately for you, I was able to do. Tigers are terrified of rats, you see.'

There was a ring of truth to all this and, feeling a little defensive,

Pilgrim decided on some retaliation, something hurtful:

'Just so I understand the linguistics,' she said in a matter-of-fact sort of a way, 'all rats are vermin but not all vermin are rats. Is that correct?'

'I'm a dumbo rat,' said the rat.

'Is that so?'

'We're distinctive for our ears being on the side of our heads and sometimes slightly bigger than normal.'

'Ears looking at you!'

You can't put a price on comedy and Pilgrim particularly enjoyed her joke.

'You seem quite careless about my identity' said the rat. 'We must hope you're not as careless about your own.'

What did the rat mean? All Pilgrim knew was that something inside her was screaming in pain.

'You're mistaking me for someone who's interested!' she replied, determined to maintain her dignified silence. But the rat continued:

'There are various sorts of rat but no doubt they all look alike to you. Yes?'

'Maybe.'

'All small and furry, so what's the difference? In your estimation, you're too important to know these things. In your little world, we don't exist as discrete entities within a shared existence. But believe me, a dumbo rat is different from the dwarf rat or albino.'

'So you keep saying, rather tediously,' said Pilgrim. 'Can I go now?'

'But fortunately for you,' continued the little creature, warming to its theme, 'the tiger also knows nothing. The tiger is big, powerful and, like you, stupid concerning rat culture. It imagines we are something to fear, which is ludicrous but served our purposes today. You're alive!'

Pilgrim stared nobly into the middle distance while feeling the sweat of shame.

'You seem suddenly closed to the truth,' said the rat.

'No – I'm just closed to you.'

'Do you fear me?'

'Fear a stupid animal? How ridiculous!'

'You'd be wiser to fear your pride, my friend. You just can't accept that you had to let go of the vine and that I helped you into that truth.'

'That has nothing to do with anything,' lied Pilgrim.

'But here's the thing: light comes not when we cling on to things but when we let go of them. There's so much to let go of!'

Pilgrim was aware of a circling presence in the sky. It was the same bird she'd seen on leaving home but she'd been mistaken about one thing: this was no hawk but an eagle, wheeling and watching, spiralling down towards them and then pulling away, high into the big hot blue. Something shiny and gold hung from its neck, which dazzled in the light.

'A big bird,' said Pilgrim.

'Dont worry yourself about the eagle,' said the rat, who was watching her.

'I'm not worried,' said Pilgrim.

'You looked troubled.'

'Not at all. The eagle is neither here nor there as far as I'm concerned. I could break its neck with a single strike.'

For the first time in her life, Pilgrim acted out a karate chop through the air.

'Not your best idea,' said the rat.

'I'm just saying. Anyway, it's you rather than me who should be scared. Eagles eat vermin.'

'My name's Veronica, by the way,' said the rat. 'And yours?'

'Pilgrim,' said Pilgrim. 'Though why you need to know who I am, I can't imagine; it's not as if we'll be meeting again.'

Like many of Pilgrim's assumptions, this proved incorrect. In fact there was so much she didn't know that, were it written down, the text would stretch from here to Mars and beyond.

The third stage

'Where am I?' wondered Pilgrim, her face pressed against a rock on which a beetle sat happily in the sun. Wherever she was she felt good. She'd slept more soundly here than she managed at home, where sleep was not always calm.

Slowly she became aware of recent events. There had been the tigers, the cliff drama and a strange meeting with a rat called Veronica. Oh, and before that, she'd been slightly rude to Consultant and Glossy Mags. And before that, she'd left behind everything she knew on some madcap journey to heaven. What had got into her?

More recently, she remembered telling the rat that she was tired and needed to sleep and the rat saying that was a good idea. But now she was awake and aware of strange noises across the plain. There was the buzz, tinkle and jangle of carousel music; the roar of lions; the coughing of seals, snorting horses, barking dogs and a crowd laughing. This could only mean one thing: she had stumbled across a circus.

'Time to relax, methinks!' said Pilgrim as she made her way towards the merriment.

'Roll up, roll up, ladeez and gennelmen!' declared a loud-voiced man with a twirly moustache, mischievous eyes, shiny top hat, frock coat and immaculate cashmere trousers. 'Headspin's Hallucinatory Mental Circus is here for your delightful delectation and utterly endless entertainment!'

On espying Pilgrim, he moved swiftly towards her.

'You, madam!'

'Yes?'

'Want a break from reality?'

'I don't know,' she said. 'I'm on my way to heaven.'

'Same thing! Your journey is over. This is heaven!'

'Really? I imagined a slightly longer quest.'

'Headspin's Hallucinatory Mental Circus is heaven on earth!'

His face was uncomfortably close and Pilgrim could smell his onion breath, but, hey ho, it takes all sorts and she'd always liked the circus. But whether this was heaven she wasn't sure. She'd no idea what heaven was like – I mean, who could possibly know that? But if heaven turned out to be a circus then, in a way, what was the point? She decided to raise the matter.

'Circuses are great fun,' she said, 'but I've never really found them very, well, useful.'

'Useful?' he said sneeringly. 'You sound like a bishop on a talk show, earnest and dull!'

The accusation hit home and left Pilgrim hot with shame.

'I didn't mean – '

'Who wants useful?!' purred onion breath. 'Lighten up, my friend! Such a pretty face should never be dull!'

'Yes, I'm sorry. I really don't want to be anything like a bishop.'

'Of course not. We don't want "useful" round here, but things twisted, clever, fascinating, intriguing and head-spinningly amazing or cruel!'

'When you put it like that – '

'So come see a man eat a live chicken,' he said, 'claws and all! You know you want to!'

Pilgrim wasn't convinced but determined to sound nothing like a bishop.

'Sounds totally groovy,' she said.

'That's more like it!' said her heavenly host. 'We don't like the serious girl!'

'The serious girl is dead,' said Pilgrim. 'Live and let live, I say! Unless you're the chicken of course.'

It must have been the rat who'd made her serious, but that was in the past. Heaven was all about having fun, surely?

'I'm having the time of my life!' she declared, and with those words Headspin – for that was his name – whisked her towards the stalls and arcades where the entertainments fought for attention.

'We're filling up nicely tonight,' he said, guiding her through the crowd with his forceful grip.

'I've never seen so many people!' said Pilgrim, happily intoxicated with the atmosphere. 'And all ripe for rowdy amusement it seems!'

'Let me explain some circus craft to you,' said Headspin, sitting her down on a bench.

'Oh, please do!'

'What brings people into the show is not what keeps them in their seats.'

'Really?'

'Oh no!'

Pilgrim loved being the pupil as this intriguing man explained the circus mysteries.

'Lions are more exciting on the hoardings than in performance,' he said.

'They attract but they can't satisfy?' said Pilgrim, enjoying her intelligent observation.

'That's what novelty's for, clever girl! It draws people in.'

'And then?'

'Who cares? You have them by then and can start to empty their pockets!'

They walked on together past the painted canopy of the carousel. Happy punters rode wooden horses, clutching twisted rods of brass while the organ blared and the money was counted. There was thrill and excitement everywhere she looked. Rifle shots cracking; hoop-la hilarity, coconut shies and the big bell sounding as another would-be strong man tried his strength with the wooden mallet.

Pilgrim was in heaven with an appetite to match. She quickly devoured the pudding and peas from Kitty's Kitchen and then moved on to her famous cherry tart and cream. And what a huge circus it was, stretching as far as the eye could see across the plain! Even now, further tents were going up beyond the entertainment; the sweaty labour of men stripped to their waists, thick-buckled belts over heaving bellies.

'It's a very big circus!' shouted Pilgrim.

'It's a world unto itself,' said Headspin. 'And we don't want anyone to leave!'

'Well, I don't want to leave. I think I could stay here for ever!'

'That's the idea!'

'There's so much going on and I don't want to miss anything!'

Headspin gazed on Pilgrim with a snake-eyed smile which she took for respect. They walked past the hot dog stall and the roasted peanut vendor with Pilgrim sampling both. Her money was running low, but who cared? This was living.

'What's the most amazing act you've ever seen?' asked Pilgrim, disciple to master.

'I've seen people stand three high on a horse,' said Headspin.

'Really?'

'Oh yes, the Fossetts did it in the Triple Jockey Act. You don't see the likes of them too often.'

'And the weirdest act?'

'The Pig-Faced lady.'

'Who was she?'

'Madame Stevens they called her, though she was in fact a brown bear whose face had been clean-shaven.'

'The Pig-Faced lady was a bear? That's quite an illusion. How was it done?'

'Simple. White gloves covered her paws with plump white arms above them.'

'Shaved?'

'Well razored, yes. She'd sit at a table in bonnet, shawl and frock, and beneath the table was a boy with a stick.'

'What did he do?'

'He'd prod her every time the showman asked a question, to make her grunt. And following each grunt, the showman would explain to the audience: 'As you see, ladies and gentlemen, the young lady understands what is said, though the peculiar formation of her jaws has deprived her of the power of uttering human speech.'

'Not quite true.'

'Nothing's true. Anyway, he'd then ask her whether she'd marry if she met the right young man.'

'How did she answer?'

'At this point, the boy would prod her harder bringing pained and angry grunts from the wretched bear.

"'All right, all right!" says the showman. "I was only asking!" – after which he passed round the hat.'

'And people believed what they saw? Had they lost their reason?'

'Reason is not a feature of the circus, my girl. Put people in a crowd and they will believe the maddest of things.'

Pilgrim did know the human herd could be stupid, but thankfully she and Headspin were above all that.

'Look around you!' he said with a sweep of his arms.

Pilgrim was aware of hundreds of people rushing.

'Folk long to be removed from their ordinary lives,' he said. 'They're aching to be plunged into the hysteria of fear, amazement or joy; anything to take them away from themselves!'

Pilgrim liked the idea of being taken away from herself, and then an amazing thought struck her.

'Perhaps I could work here?' she ventured.

'You?' said Headspin, looking her over with fresh interest.

'Why not?' said Pilgrim, surprised to hear herself saying these things but quite unable to stop.

Her short visit to the circus had made her realise something: how very dull her life was. Perhaps that's why she'd thought of a journey to heaven in the first place, just to escape the tedium of herself. Perhaps all this talk of heaven was just a superstition unhappy people needed to believe in.

'Do you believe in heaven?' asked Pilgrim.

'Who needs heaven when you can live in the circus?' said Headspin, with slight discomfort. Not that Pilgrim noticed, because you stop noticing things in the Mental Circus. There's just too much going on to be mindful of anything but the next amazing event.

'And who needs friends like Veronica,' thought Pilgrim, 'when you can have a teacher like Headspin, the dark and dangerous High Priest of distraction?'

'Can you juggle?' asked Headspin.

He was clearly keen she should work there.

'Is this an interview?' said Pilgrim excitedly.

'Could be, young lady.'

'Well, I can't really juggle, no. I can do one apple but more than that – '

'Then perhaps you can leap from a trapeze?'

'Heights are a problem.'

'You could work with the animals.'

'Why not? I used to have a dog!'

'Ahh! So you could train the wild lions and put a tutu on a cheetah?'

'The dog was a Labrador. Lions and cheetahs would be upping my game a little.'

'I'm sure we could find a place for you somewhere.'

'Oh, thank you!'

'As long as you're able to pay.'

'Pay?'

'Of course! This isn't a charity, you stupid fool!'

The atmosphere grew cold, like the sudden chill of a dark cloud crossing the sun.

'Stupid?' said Pilgrim.

She didn't like her new hero calling her stupid.

'It's just a word,' said Headspin dismissively.

'And "fool"?'

'Just another word.'

'Not very nice words,' said Pilgrim. 'And I can't pay because I've got no money left. I've spent it all here.'

'You've got no money?'

'Not a penny!'

'Then stop wasting my time!'

'Wasting your time?'

'People like you make me sick!'

'But I thought we were friends?'

'Friends? Here in the circus we perform the clever, the fascinating, the amazing and the cruel! We don't perform friendship. You're nothing to me and I've got a circus to run.'

'But we were having such an interesting conversation!'

Suddenly his face was pressed close to hers.

'You'd be surprised how easily I move on to the next thing. I suggest you do the same.'

And with that, Headspin pulled away and strode off into the distance, soon lost in the heaving mass of the deceived.

Pilgrim didn't know what to do. She'd spent all her money on rides which simply took her round and round in circles and then dumped her back where she'd started. It had seemed exciting at the time but left both her pockets and soul feeling bare. She felt cold in the chill circus air. Wandering away from the crowd, she found a dark corner and there, heavy with despair, she sat down on a colourful sofa, now discarded.

'Ahgghh!'

Pilgrim jumped up with surprise. The groan wasn't hers. It sounded a little like an old boyfriend but he was now in Australia, so that didn't fit. And beyond the question 'who?' was the question: 'why?' Why would anyone be groaning in a circus? The circus was a happy place, surely? You groan at the dentist or during long sermons but not at the circus which is a place of hilarity and thrill. She peered into the dark but could see no one.

'I must have imagined it,' she thought, as she sat down again.

'Ooauugghh!'

No, she hadn't imagined that! It was a definite groan, louder than before and came from the colourful sofa, which on closer inspection turned out to be a clown, lying on the ground.

'I'm very sorry,' said Pilgrim. 'I thought you were a colourful sofa.'

'No, I'm a sad clown.'

'But you're smiling.'

'It's make-up.'

'Of course,' she said, feeling a fool. 'I'm learning there's not very much that's real in a circus. I'm Pilgrim, by the way, and I'm on my way to heaven.'

'That sounds nice.'

'It's not all cake and roses, believe me,' she said, remembering the tigers. 'But tell me: why are you lying on the ground when you should be making the children laugh.'

'You don't want to know.'

'I do want to know.'

'I tried to leave the circus,' he said.

The clown held his side as he talked. His breathing was clearly painful.

'So?' said Pilgrim, confused.

'They didn't like it.'

'Who didn't like it?'

'Don't get involved.'

'I am involved, and stop trying to push me away.' said Pilgrim. 'What's the problem with you leaving?'

'They don't like you to leave.'

'Everyone can leave!'

'Can they?'

Pilgrim's words dried in her mouth when she saw the clown's bruised head.

'So what happened?' she asked.

'Headspin had me roughed over.'

'Roughed over?'

'Knocked about by the men over there.'

Pilgrim looked with new eyes at the bare-bellied men erecting the tents. She'd imagined them to be cheerful chappies but there was clearly a darker side. She noticed also that they were now throwing stones at the sky.

'They do what they're told,' said the clown.

'So what are they doing now?'

'They're trying to scare the eagle away.'

'I've seen that eagle before.'

'A fine bird!'

'I suppose so.'

'They hate that bird.'

'Not a nice bunch, I grant you and I'm sorry they treated you in this manner. But tell me – why do you want to leave?'

'I'm called Mr Happy.'

'A good name and everyone loves you for it.'

'But what if Mr Happy is sad?'

'Sad?'

'I think I'm sad.'

'You're not sure?'

'I haven't been allowed to feel for so long it's hard to be sure. But I think it's sadness that wakes me up at night.'

'Well, that's not very good, is it? No one wants to see a sad clown. Let me try and cheer you up.'

'I don't want to be cheered up.'

'Why ever not?'

'I just want to be allowed to feel the sadness for a while.'

'No one should feel sad,' said Pilgrim, who liked to provide solutions for other people, even if she couldn't do it for herself. 'I won't allow it!'

'Everyone must visit the Garden of Sadness sometime, my friend,' said Happy. 'So will you help me get out of here so I can feel again?'

Pilgrim looked nervously across at the muscle-bound tent men.

'Of course I will.'

The men were very large.

'I mean, obviously I can't take sides in this dispute,' she added on grounds of health and safety; her own. 'I see myself more as a facilitator.'

Oh no, had she really said that? She was beginning to sound like Con.

'You are taking sides, Pilgrim, and I have a plan.'

Pilgrim was taken aback at such a firm intervention from Mr Happy.

'What's happened to your voice?' she asked. 'It appears to have gone up three octaves. Is it the stress?'

'That wasn't my voice,' said Mr Happy.

'Then whose voice was it?' asked Pilgrim.

'It was mine,' said Veronica.

'Are you stalking me?'

But with the help of Pilgrim and Veronica, Mr Happy did manage to escape Headspin's Hallucinatory Mental Circus. They found a false moustache, dressed him in Pilgrim's coat and, at the key moment, Veronica distracted the gate keeper by running up his trouser leg.

'There's a ferret up my trousers!' he screamed, and in the ensuing confusion Pilgrim and Happy slipped through the gates and merged with the drifting crowd beyond the turnstiles. Veronica joined them soon after, a little shaken but unscathed.

Pilgrim then thought of a really good joke.

'How was the last leg of the journey?' she asked Veronica.

'Surprisingly hairy.'

'I don't want to know any more,' said Pilgrim.

They walked together in silence across the plain. When they looked back, the circus had moved on, leaving only litter and trampled grass. Veronica noticed Pilgrim's surprise.

'The mental circus comes and goes,' she said.

'But it seemed so real,' said Pilgrim.

'It seems very real when you're caught up in it.'

'Thank you,' said Happy as he breathed the air of freedom.

'It was a pleasure,' said Veronica. 'I heard you were trying to leave.'

'I didn't tell anyone.'

'You told yourself. That's enough.'

'That's what they said to me,' added Pilgrim, remembering the removal man's words. '"We heard you were trying to leave," he said. The man even claimed I'd made a phone call.'

'Which man?' asked Happy.

'Called himself Will Good,' said Pilgrim. 'But if my experience is anything to go by, be careful what you wish for. What do you wish for, by the way?'

'I don't know,' said Happy. 'But I know what I don't wish for.'

And sometimes, of course, that's enough.

The fourth stage

Somewhere inside, Pilgrim was dreading her farewell to Happy. 'It would have been nice to have company on the journey to heaven,' she said.

'There's always company on the journey,' said Veronica, 'but you travel alone.'

'Alone but in company?'

'That's right.'

'I have to say that sounds pretty odd,' said Pilgrim.

Happy, however, seemed to understand the idea better.

'The thing is, Pilgrim, you have to find happiness in yourself. You can't expect someone to bring it to your door. That never works.'

'That's rich coming from one who's paid to bring happiness to others!' said Pilgrim.

'No, I don't bring them happiness. I merely find the happiness already there.'

'And if it isn't there?'

'I grant you, it's well hidden sometimes!'

'But I still don't understand why the tent men turned against you,' said Pilgrim.

'They did what they were told.'

'Told by who?'

'By Headspin.'

'And what was his problem?'

'I hope you won't be offended but I was Headspin's boyfriend.'

'Oh!'

Pilgrim wasn't at all offended but she was surprised, which

made her voice come out higher than she wished. Surprise then gave way to concern and some anger.

'And he had you beaten up? That's a big falling out. What happened?'

'I started to convene a little group of circus folk.'

'Like who?'

'Jenny Trapeze, Horseman Harry, Lionel the Lion Tamer, all sorts. They were all unhappy in different ways. So once a week we'd sit silent in a circle and try to remember what we'd been before we joined the circus; and what we wanted to be when we left.'

'I like that idea.'

'Headspin didn't. When he found out, well, that was it.'

'He didn't like the silence?'

'Hated it. Always tried to fill it. He didn't like people stopping, you see. It made him angry.'

'So what happened?'

'We were sitting there quietly one day when the lynch mob burst in and removed each of us for separate retribution.'

'How do you mean?'

'They made Jenny perform a catch on the trapeze with greased hands and no safety net. She fell.'

'That's hateful!'

'Harry was dragged across a field by his horses, deliberately frightened by gun fire. And you don't want to hear what happened to Lionel. I was lucky to get away with a beating, believe me.'

Pilgrim was in a state of shock.

'You were certainly taken in by Headspin,' she said.

'Yes, I was.

There was a pause.

'Just like you were, Pilgrim.'

'Me?'

'Hook, line and sinker.'

'He never fooled me for a moment!'

'Really?'

'No, I read people,' said Pilgrim, a little flustered. 'They're like an open book to me.'

'Of course they are,' said Happy. 'How did it go? "That's groovy, Mr Headspin! Oh, I'd love to work here, Mr Headspin! We're such good friends, Mr Headspin! Oh, three bags full Mr Headspin, sir!"'

Happy's impersonation of Pilgrim was painfully accurate and Veronica was aching with mirth.

'Well, he may have fooled me for a moment,' said Pilgrim, looking firmly at her feet.

'The good news is, it doesn't matter any more,' said Happy. 'Headspin has no power over either of us now.'

'That's true.'

They walked for a while with that awareness.

'There are no authority figures in the world,' said Veronica. 'Just a lot of people who pretend authority. So don't let anyone fool you.'

And with that, she was gone, leaving Pilgrim and Happy alone.

'That's quite a thought,' said Pilgrim. 'No authority figures? I like it!'

'But there are one or two who possess authority,' said Happy.

'You mean real authority?'

'Indeed. And they're worth finding.'

They walked on further, Happy enjoying his freedom and Pilgrim thinking about authority figures who could be trusted.

'It's hard to recognise them,' said Pilgrim.

'It is at first.'

'I mean, you were Headspin's boyfriend! So how fooled were you?'

'I was young,' said Happy with a resigned sigh. 'Back then, I didn't know who I was, so how could I know about anyone else? And over time I allowed myself to become defined by another person, which is never a good idea.'

'No.'

'And the thing is, I don't want to be defined by someone else again, Pilgrim, which is why I must leave you.'

'Leave me? I thought we could travel together.'

'My path isn't yours.'

'I suppose not,' she said, with disappointment. 'But perhaps we'll meet along the way.'

'Possible. We'll exchange notes.'

'That's right. Different journeys can sometimes coincide for a while. Separate but gladly relating!'

'Separate but gladly relating,' said Happy. 'That's good, Pilgrim. And I'll always be grateful you sat on me, of course.'

'I thought you were a colourful sofa,' she said, explaining herself once again.

'I understand – really!'

'And though you say you're grateful now, you did groan a lot at the time.'

'Oh, me of little faith!' chuckled Happy. 'I'd asked for help; it just wasn't the help I expected.'

They shared a smile of recognition. They'd both made their plans and both seen their plans ripped up.

'We don't know anything, do we?' said Pilgrim, reflecting on the fact that her own journey started when she slipped and fell down the stairs.

'We know that we don't know,' said Happy, 'and perhaps that's enough for true adventurers.'

The journey to heaven offered wonderful banter along the way and Pilgrim had enjoyed being part of Happy's salvation. But when they reached a Crossroad of Decision, one path came for him and another came for Pilgrim. They said their goodbyes and took their different paths.

'If we do meet again,' said Pilgrim, 'I'll make no attempt to define you!'

'Agreed!' shouted Happy. 'But for now: alone yet in company!'

And then he was gone. As she watched him go and contemplated the path ahead, Pilgrim did wonder if they'd ever meet again.

The fifth stage

Pilgrim followed a tall old wall for a while and felt more alone than was good for her happiness. She paused for a moment to make an entry in her diary:

> *I liked Happy and would have enjoyed sharing my adventure with him. I feel he knows a bit more than me; that despite being a clown, he's further ahead on the journey. It's stupid we have to part, he could have helped me. I don't miss Veronica, who may be stalking me, which is illegal. Hopefully she won't bother me again.*

On resuming her travels, Pilgrim met no one along the way except the shadowy figure of a small girl.

'Is that a ghost?' wondered Pilgrim.

The ghostly girl would watch her from the bushes or loiter on the path ahead as though wanting attention or desiring to talk. But Pilgrim had no time for conversation with a stray child and averted her eyes.

'People should look after their children more,' thought Pilgrim as she continued to follow the large wall. 'Here she is, trying to attract the attention of a stranger! Anything could happen! I blame the parents.'

Leaving the girl behind, she began to wonder what lay behind the wall. On reaching a small gate she peered eagerly inside, and what a sight! Beyond the gate lay an autumn garden, a watercolour wash of orange, red and yellow gold. Drawn to its beauty, Pilgrim was pushing at the gate when there was a sudden voice in her ear.

'Don't don't don't don't don't don't don't don't don't!'

'I beg your pardon?' said Pilgrim.

'Don't don't don't don't don't don't don't don't don't!'

Pilgrim felt the need to be firm.

'When I said 'I beg your pardon', I was asking you to explain yourself not repeat everything.'

But the visitor was not to be deterred.

'Really young lady, don't don't don't don't don't don't don't don't don't!'

Pilgrim gazed on the figure before her. He was the most breathless and egg-shaped human she'd ever seen.

'Are you a priest?' she asked.

'A priest? Why do you think I'm a priest?'

'That's twenty-seven "don'ts" before you know who I am. The clues are there.'

'I'm not a priest, no, but you'll be grateful, believe me,' said the Egg.

'So what's your name?'

'I'm Breathless and Terrified.'

'I can see that, but what's your name?'

'No, that is my name.'

'Breathless and Terrified?'

'That's right. It's a double-barrelled name with "and" in the middle to help it flow off the tongue.'

'Breathless and Terrified. It does sort of flow.'

'I was terribly teased at school before adding the "and"'.

Pilgrim felt it was time to move on.

'So tell me: why all the "don'ts"'?

'Isn't it obvious?'

'Not to me.'

'You were about to push open the gate and walk inside the garden!'

'True. It's very beautiful.'

'Are you mad?'

'I don't think so. I'm on the journey to heaven.'

'Well, you won't find it in there, missy! That's the last place you'll find it.'

This sounded strange to Pilgrim.

'I can see your fear, Breathless but I can't see the cause. It's like seeing smoke without fire. Am I missing something? Why is this garden so terrifying?'

Breathless and Terrified tried to calm down but failed. He was breathless and terrified by name and nature.

'I keep myself busy, that's what I do,' he said.

'Why?' asked Pilgrim.

'Don't let the water still, that's the secret! Keep stirring the water! Keep stirring the water! If you let the water still, you see reality and you don't want that, you so don't! That's why I keep myself busy, because if I didn't – '

'Yes?'

'I'd end up doing what you were about to do!'

'Enter the garden?'

'Oh don't say it, don't even say it!'

'It's that bad?'

'It would just be the worst thing ever. In fact, excuse me a minute!'

Sweating and shaking, Breathless and Terrified reached inside a pocket as if for medication. His twitchy hands pulled out some technology and he played with it for a while.

'I can do everything on this!' he said excitedly.

After a while, he began to calm, as one drugged.

'That's better,' he muttered and then returned the technology to his pocket.

'What was that all about?' asked Pilgrim.

'I just needed to keep the waters stirred. Twenty-four-hour connection to everything!'

'Except yourself.'

'Who wants to connect with themselves?' said the Egg. 'That's wholly inadvisable.'

'Why? Isn't reality a good thing?'

'Ssshhh!'

'Sssshh? Why the ssshhh? Have I stumbled upon a forbidden word?'

'Too much reality and I begin to drift towards the – '

'The what?'

'The Garden of Sadness.'

Breathless and Terrified nodded nervously towards the gate.

'So this is the Garden of Sadness?' said Pilgrim.

'Where I just know I'd crack open and disintegrate completely.'

Pilgrim paused for a moment. This was the place recommended by Happy, so why the terror?

'Everyone cracks sometime,' said Pilgrim. 'I mean, what would someone be if they didn't crack sometime?'

'Not me, not me!' said Breathless. 'Sadness brings tears as surely as a well-keeper draws water. And cracking up like that is totally the worst thing in the world.'

'But if you're crying on the inside, why not on the outside?'

'It's different for men,' said Breathless dismissively. 'You wouldn't understand. Women cry at a cat in the rain. But men? We can't behave like that. Now, I really must go. Just the sight of the place – '

He looked with terror at the garden once again.

'Agghh!'

With that, Breathless and Terrified scuttled off down the road, leaving Pilgrim with a dilemma. The garden looked inviting, full of sweeping autumn vistas. But set against this, Breathless had called it 'the Garden of Sadness' and displayed only terror in its presence. If the truth be known, Pilgrim didn't feel like cracking up either.

At that moment, the butterfly reappeared. It seemed to greet her, fluttering around her head in a mad and flappy way before heading through the gate and into the garden. Pilgrim watched but remained stationary, unable to move. The Egg's terror had left its scar.

'*Breathless and Terrified has just left in a big sweat of fear,*' she noted in her diary. '*He's a bit condescending and ignorant but it's true in a way – it's important to stay in control of things. So what's a girl to do?*'

Pilgrim was erring on the side of caution.

'Perhaps I should continue along the wall and stay away from the garden itself,' she said to herself.

She'd made her choice when the butterfly reappeared. It had returned to find her and now flapped around Pilgrim's head and feet, causing her to hop and jump as if the creature found her stationary pose offensive.

And so, when the butterfly again headed through the gate, Pilgrim followed. On the journey to heaven, you don't argue with a butterfly.

The sixth stage

The garden was haunted by beauty. The smell of pine cones and apple trees lingered in the air and a gentle mist shimmered in the embers of the dying sun. It should have been the best walk of her life.

'If I'd imagined my favourite place on earth,' thought Pilgrim, 'this is how it would be!'

Yet strangely, a dull stupor of spirit came over her at this time, denying peace and joy. With each step of the way, she became more enclosed in her self and more resistant to everything that was fine and wonderful around her. In the end, she sat down by a large rock and shouted in a loud voice:

'This is ridiculous!'

'How so, my friend?' came the reply.

'I just need to be alone,' said Pilgrim.

She didn't have to look, she recognised the voice. Veronica was sitting on top of the rock, three feet above her head,

'What in you resists the beauty?' she asked.

'I'm not resisting the beauty,' said Pilgrim. 'I can see it!'

'But you can't feel it. When you're ready, it might be good to crack a little and let the tears out.'

'No need for that,' said Pilgrim, determined to stay dry-eyed. 'I'm fine.'

'"Fine" as in frantic insecure neurotic and emotional?'

'No "fine" as in "just leave me alone!"'

'You're allowed to be sad,' observed Veronica.

Pilgrim didn't want to be sad. She just wanted to get to heaven and be happy for ever and ever. But she couldn't deny the reaction Veronica's words triggered inside her. So many regrets, so many 'if onlys' in her life, and somehow they all seemed trapped in her body, unmourned and numbing joy.

'Sometimes we do unforgivable things because that's all we can do,' said Veronica.

'Why don't you just leave me alone!?' said Pilgrim in a sudden fit of rage.

She liked to think of herself as a peaceable figure but her temper could at times erupt like a volcano and destroy all around. Veronica had it coming.

'I will leave you alone.'

'Good.'

'And I'm glad you're angry,' said Veronica.

'Oh, I can get much angrier than this!' said Pilgrim. 'I'm so angry now I could pull down this whole wretched world; bring it crashing to the ground in ruins!'

'And that's allowed,' said Veronica, unmoved by the eruption. 'We need proper anger to reach proper sadness.'

'Proper sadness? I'm on the path to heaven not sadness.'

'Let me tell you something, Pilgrim,' said Veronica, wiping some dust from her whiskers.

'Please don't,' said Pilgrim, who had never liked being told anything.

'The goal of life,' said Veronica, 'is to become who we are, to know ourselves fully and to be fully known.'

'I know who I am.'

'No, most of you is unknown, Pilgrim, like an unopened letter.'

'Is this going somewhere?'

'You told Breathless that cracks let in light.'

'True.'

'But you forgot to mention that you're as frightened of the cracks as he is!'

Pilgrim was most offended.

'For your information, Ratty, I'm the most self-aware person I know!'

'Then you must have the address book of a hermit.'

There was an awkward pause.

'I must go,' said Veronica, 'but before I do, let me tell you one more circus story.'

'I've had enough of the circus for a lifetime,' said Pilgrim, still coming to terms with how fooled she'd been.

'In the nineteenth century,' said Veronica, 'there was a midget called Tom Thumb. He was twenty-five inches tall and weighed fifteen pounds.'

'What has this got to do with me?' said Pilgrim. 'It's you who has height issues.'

Her disdain for this creature knew no bounds.

'So at the age of seven,' continued Veronica, 'having stopped growing at six months, he was smaller than a one-year-old child.'

'And your point is?'

'Barnum, the great showman and entertainer, saw the chance to make some money. He signed up Tom Thumb for a tour of Europe. But in order to make it profitable he persuaded the public to pay a shilling to see him rather than a penny.'

'How?'

'Pre-publicity! He built up the image of Tom in the public imagination. He was the most amazing sight on earth, the most intriguing individual on earth!'

'So the hype worked? That's advertising for you.'

'In a way it did, but unfortunately for Barnum it wasn't just the public who believed the hype; Tom Thumb believed it too. He was built up in his own imagination and became unbearably pompous and overbearing to such an extent that even Barnum could not handle him.'

There was a silence in the garden.

'Please go,' said Pilgrim. 'Before I crush you.'

'I'm gone,' said Veronica inching her way down the rock towards undergrowth. 'But should the white doves come,' she said turning back for a moment.

'What white doves?'

'Should the white doves come, Pilgrim, allow them, love them and throw each into the air with a loud goodbye. They long to fly free!'

'A *bad day just got worse*,' wrote Pilgrim in her diary. '*Some nonsense about white doves. File under "gobbledygook".*'

Later that day Pilgrim was looking for a way out of the garden; she'd had enough of the place.

'I wish I'd listened to Breathless,' she thought. 'This isn't right for me. I'm on a higher spiritual plane than other people. They just don't understand.'

She was restless by the river, thinking dark thoughts about rats and wondering what Veronica had meant when she spoke of white doves coming.

'Probably more psychobabble!' she decided.

And the child wasn't helping. Yes, the ghost child had reappeared on a carpet of red and orange leaves in the wood. She skipped a little and ran in circles around a big oak tree. She wanted Pilgrim to play, but Pilgrim wasn't in the mood. She was ruminating again on the child's parents when the girl ran across into a wood. Pilgrim followed. If the child was going home she'd take the opportunity to give someone a helpful lecture about child care.

'Parents!'

But on emerging from the trees, Pilgrim forgot all about parents, for there on the river bank was Breathless and Terrified, surrounded by white doves!

'Hello there!' he said cheerfully.

'Hello, Breathless!' said Pilgrim, stunned.

This was not the frightened shell of former times. Instead, Breathless sat at peace with a hundred cracks across his person and spilling from each crack, a tear. His whole body was crying with relief.

'What are you doing here?' asked Pilgrim. 'I thought the Garden of Sadness was the last place you wished to be.'

'It was,' said Breathless. 'But when you have to come here, they have to let you in.'

'And you had to come?'

'Apparently so. I'm not sure what happened. But I do know I was bored of my unhappiness and somehow that overcame my terror of the garden.'

It was hard to see Breathless for the doves that cooed around him.

'And your feathered friends?'

'You'll never believe this.'

'Try me.'

'Well, as I named each sadness, each failure and regret, I felt a crack in my shell.'

'Really?'

'And then from each crack, a tear would break free.'

'Your body was crying?'

'And wherever the tear landed, a white dove would appear like a – well, like a witness, I suppose. So I'm not short of feathered friends!'

'True.'

'Though what happens now, I'm not sure. I mean, what do I do with them all?'

One of the braver doves was perched on his head and two more sat either side on his shoulders. Pilgrim, who'd once had an unfortunate experience with seagulls, wasn't sure this was ideal.

'I might be able to help,' she said.

'Really?'

'You throw each dove in the air with a loud goodbye and watch them fly away.'

'How do you know?' asked Breathless.

'A friend told me; well, an acquaintance. One can hardly call a rat a friend.'

'Wonderful!' said Breathless and Terrified who now needed a change of name. 'Then that's what I'll do!'

Pilgrim stayed for a while as a laughing Breathless cast each bird into the air and watched it soar up, up and away.

'I haven't been this happy since ever!' he shouted.

He was still going strong as darkness fell and ever more visible as light flooded from the cracks in his shattered shell. There on the river bank, he was like a particularly bright glow-worm. It was the death of Breathless and Terrified yet could hardly have been a more joyful occasion.

Pilgrim meanwhile withdrew into the shadows of her own soul. Thankfully, the child was nowhere to be seen.

The seventh stage

Pilgrim had never felt better. How long had she been in the Garden of Sadness? She wasn't sure but as she looked ahead there was a huge field of sunflowers bordered by a wood. Truly she was happy to be herself today! This was how she felt. The angry pilgrim of before had given way to a pilgrim open to adventure and slightly troubled by the way she had spoken to Veronica.

'*Dear Diary*,' she wrote. '*Note about spiritual people. A spiritual person is one who enjoys all the flowers along the path but also grasps the nettle. I'll need to apologise to Veronica.*'

The rat was irritating but she had been right about the doves and Pilgrim hoped that wasn't their last meeting.

And then a most curious sight as out of the wood and through the sunflowers came a thin man dancing. He was serenading a stone which he held in his hands. He wore the thickest of round glasses which made him peer and squint. He looked up towards the sun, danced a little more and then held his finger to the wind. Seemingly satisfied, he placed the stone on a log. Pilgrim watched as he removed his glasses, wiped them on his sleeve, returned them to his pointy nose and adjusted the position of the stone slightly. It seemed to matter which way the stone was pointing.

Pilgrim was intrigued by this figure in baggy trousers and braces dancing his way through a task which she found hard to comprehend. Neither could she hear the music to which the man moved. It was like watching a ballet with no sound.

Pilgrim decided on a cheery hello.

'Hello!' she called out and began to walk towards him.

'What are you so cheery about?' asked the dancing man.

'And what are you so grumpy about?' asked Pilgrim.

'I have to start again after losing my last job,' said the man with the pointy nose. 'That's why I'm a bit grumpy.'

'And I'm standing next to the most wonderful field of sunflowers I've ever seen,' said Pilgrim. 'And that's why I'm so cheery. My name is Pilgrim, by the way.'

'And mine is Pointy,' said the man, which cast a cloud over Pilgrim's high spirits, for this was surely cruel?

Yes of course he had a pointed nose. Pilgrim could not remember a nose quite so sharp in her entire life. Here was a real balloon-buster of a snout. But in Pilgrim's eyes, odd physical attributes should not determine your name. That was playground savagery which should not pass into adult life.

'I'm very sorry,' said Pilgrim with genuine concern.

'What for?'

'That is a cruel name and one which is quite untrue.'

'What are you talking about?' asked Pointy, peering up from his stone.

'Your nose,' said Pilgrim. 'It's a very nice nose with absolutely nothing wrong with it. I've seen noses much more pointed than yours. Not many, but some.'

Pointy removed his glasses, polished them again and returned them to his nose.

'He thinks not well who thinks not twice,' he said.

'I beg your pardon?'

'My name has nothing to do with my nose,' he said.

Pilgrim managed to nod in a manner to suggest this went without saying.

'Just as I thought,' she mumbled.

Pilgrim tried not to look at Pointy's conk while hoping for an explanation.

'I give directions,' said Pointy. 'I used to be a dancer but now I point people in the right direction. Hence 'Pointy'.

'Oh I see. You're a guide?'

'Loosely speaking and in a general and non-specific sort of

way.'

'Well, I'm glad of a guide right now as I'm trying to leave the Garden of Sadness,' said Pilgrim.

'Yes, I know. That's why the stone is in place. You'll be aware that I took some care over that.'

Pilgrim looked down at the stone and, as she followed its line, there appeared on the horizon a large arch and gate in the garden wall.

'That's your gate,' said Pointy.

'I'm not sure it is,' said Pilgrim. 'It's not the one I came in by.'

'It wouldn't be.'

'Why not?'

'Those who enter the Garden of Sadness never leave by the same gate.'

'Oh, I see. Yes, that makes sense. It was a butterfly who guided me here.'

'Billie?'

'She didn't give her name. Orange and blue.'

'Definitely Billie. She's part-time like me. I'm here now to point you to the desert,' he said.

'The desert?' said Pilgrim.

But Pointy had already broken out into another dance. Pilgrim watched him for a while until he became breathless and fell over, mid-pirouette. He wasn't as young as once he was, though in truth there aren't many who are.

'So how did you know I was here?' asked Pilgrim, helping him up.

'How could I miss you with all those doves?'

'Ah, the doves!'

Yes, Pilgrim had herself cracked soon after leaving Breathless, though the whys and the wherefores remained a mystery.

'I saw you throwing one after another into the air,' said Pointy, 'so I knew something was up.'

'Yes, there were a lot of doves.'

'And a lot of light! You were like a bonfire in the dark.'

'I've never been as happy as when I was throwing those doves into the air.'

'So tell me,' said Pointy conspiratorially, 'do you hear the music?'

'The music?'

Pilgrim listened carefully, hoping to catch Beethoven's Fifth on the wind.

'I'm not sure.'

'You'd know if you did.'

'Then perhaps I don't,' she said sadly.

'That's all right,' said Pointy. 'It was a long time before I heard it. You can only do your best.'

'But what if my best isn't good enough?'

'Your best is always good enough. And if you can't do your best, your half-best is fine.'

'Quarter-best?'

'Quarter-best is perfect.'

Pilgrim was relieved to hear this. Quarter-best was about her level.

'Well, time waits for no man and I must be on my way,' said the former dancer, 'but before I go, I ask one favour.'

'What's that?'

'Give my regards to Word Shy if you meet him.'

'Word Shy? Who's that?'

'It's not his real name, just what we call him. He's a shepherd in the desert.'

'Word Shy?'

'That's right.'

'The name's ironic, I suppose,' said Pilgrim, sensing a laugh. 'Like a zebra called 'Spot'. The man's a verbal machine gun?'

'Quite the opposite,' said Pointy. 'He doesn't say anything.'

'Nothing? You mean he's dumb?'

'He's not dumb but something happened. He went away, though no one's sure where. Some say to war, others say to another land or just further into the desert. But whatever he did and whatever he saw, when he returned it was different. He believes he has only seven words to speak before he dies.'

'Only seven?'

'That's right.'

'I can see why he's word shy!'

'Now if you had seven words, what would you say?'

Pilgrim wondered silently.

'Anyway, give him my best,' said Pointy.

And with that, Pointy glided away, waltzing through the sunflowers leaving behind only the aroma of his expensive aftershave and the stone pointing towards the gate. Pilgrim took a last look around the Garden of Sadness and decided it was poorly named.

'You should be the Garden of Joy!' she said to no one, as she started towards the gate. Beyond the gate, and waiting for her in all its sun-baked glory, was the desert.

The eighth stage

Pilgrim gazed down upon a desert plain dominated by a vast rock. It was enormous in size, frightening to behold and profoundly ancient. Geological eras had come and gone in the formation of this towering edifice. Petrified rivulets covered its hard bronze surface which became black in the shadow. Twisted towers of granite rose high in the sky, the buckled offspring of shifting tectonic plates below. It was enormous and impassable and would make a demanding climb.

'*I'm looking at a ridiculously large mountain,*' wrote Pilgrim in her diary. '*I have absolutely no idea what it is but it presents itself like a monster with whom I must do business. That's my first impression. Hopefully I'm wrong and it's just for tourists. Or perhaps I can go round it or avoid it completely.*'

But Pilgrim viewed the mountain with growing fear, for as she peered into the distance, she saw her path led towards it and then stopped.

'So what happens when I reach the rock?' she wondered to herself. 'Will my journey to heaven require me to become a mountaineer?'

She was about to set off towards it when she heard a voice. It was not a strong voice; indeed like a soft tyre, it had a deflated air and seemed to be spoken through someone's nose.

'If you've got any sense,' said the nose voice, 'you'll avoid that horrible mountain.'

Pilgrim turned round to see a round-shouldered individual, trying to light a fire and failing.

'The fire doesn't light like it used to,' said a human so lacking in substance that Pilgrim could almost see through him.

'Who are you?' said Pilgrim.

'My name's Chill-Out.'

'I see. And your friend?'

Pilgrim was aware of a woman of indeterminate age lying on a slab of stone. She had beads in her hair and gazed into the big blue sky. Pilgrim was wondering about their relationship when the bead woman spoke:

'You've just got to move on,' she said without moving.

Pilgrim looked quizzically at Chill-Out. What was she talking about? But Chill-Out was in a trance of adoration.

'That's Move-On,' said Chill-Out, shaking his head in awe and wonder. 'She's a true prophet.'

'Is she?' said Pilgrim, unconvinced. She'd never met a prophet but if she did she hoped they'd be a little more impressive than this.

'Total prophet, man,' confirmed Chill-Out.

'And what's her great message?' asked Pilgrim.

'She tells people to move on.'

'Really?'

'Totally prophetic.'

Pilgrim reflected on the thin line between 'prophetic' and 'pathetic' but kept her thoughts to herself.

'Well, I am moving on,' said Pilgrim. 'I'm on a journey to heaven so our prophet should be pleased.'

'A journey where?' asked Chill-Out.

'I'm on a journey to heaven and it looks like my next task is to face that enormous rock which so dominates the sky line. Any ideas as to what it might be?'

'Just move on,' said Move-On, again without shifting.

'Is she listening to me?' asked Pilgrim testily. 'I just said I was moving on.'

'Chill out, brother,' said Chill-Out. 'Calm the negative energy. Move-On doesn't need to listen.'

'She doesn't need to listen?' said Pilgrim with some surprise.

'Oh, I see. Well, that's quite a gift.'

'Yes, she's on a different level of consciousness and speaks from what we call "The Enchanted Place".'

'And how do you get to this Enchanted Place?' enquired Pilgrim.

'You just move on,' said the immobile prophet.

Something was getting on Pilgrim's nerves, ever so slightly.

'You don't seem to be doing much moving yourself,' she said.

'You don't understand,' said Chill-Out, who was apparently the prophet's spokesman on Planet Earth. 'It's not about moving on as such.'

'I see.'

'It's more about avoiding things. It's about avoiding all the bad stuff you don't want to face. Like the enormous Rock of Hidden Self.'

'Ah? So that's what it's called.'

Pilgrim looked at the mountain with new eyes. The Rock of Hidden Self? Her initial fears seemed well founded.

'You just, like, avoid it, man. Pretend it isn't there.'

'And that's moving on, is it?'

'It's a new consciousness.'

'It sounds really great,' said Pilgrim.

'It is really great,' confirmed Chill-Out. 'It's really, really great.'

'I was being ironic,' said Pilgrim. 'How can you move on from something unless you first face it?'

'Well – '

'How can you say goodbye to something until you've said hello? That's spiritual by-passing. You two haven't moved on from the rock, you've just run away from it.'

Chill-Out clearly felt harassed and started shaking.

'You don't need to go hissy on me!' he said.

'I'm not going "hissy" on you,' said Pilgrim, 'whatever that means. But – and tell me if I'm wrong – what I'm sensing is this: "move on" seems to be a polite word for denial.'

'You just move on,' said Move-On from the enchanted place.

Suddenly something made sense.

'I see now!' said Pilgrim. 'That explains why you're prisoners here.'

'Prisoners?' said Chill-Out. 'We're not prisoners, man, we're, like, free!'

'No, you're prisoners. For some reason, you don't want to visit the rock.'

A look of fear moved across Chill-Out's face.

'Negative vibes,' he said. 'We tried to walk round it but you can't do that. So we live here now.'

If Pilgrim was honest, an occasional occurrence, she was sounding more confident than she felt. She looked towards the rock which stood in her way and felt only a dull terror. Like Chill-Out, she wanted to walk round it or like the immobile Move-On, lie on a stone, gaze at the sky all day and call it 'The Enchanted Place'. In fact she was warming to the idea of staying when Billie the Butterfly returned, fluttering past her and out into the desert towards the rock.

'You just want to move on,' said the prophet, dreamily.

'And that's what I'm going to do,' said Pilgrim. 'Cheerio, Chill-Out.'

'Peace, man.'

'I'm a woman.'

'Peace, woman.'

'Thank you. But I suspect there can be no peace until I've faced the rock.'

And with that she started to walk. Scrambling down from the rock, one foot was placed in the sand and then another, for this is how journeys work.

'You can't always get everywhere suddenly,' said Pilgrim to herself.

And then remembering what Will Good said, she added, 'You just trust the path and keep on walking.'

She looked back only once. Chill-Out had returned to the fire he'd never lit while Move-On had moved nowhere.

The ninth stage

There was good news and bad news as Pilgrim approached the rock, and we start with the bad: there was no path other than the path to the rock. Like the open jaws of a killer whale, the mighty mass drew everything towards it. Pilgrim now understood how Chill-Out and Move-On had been unable to avoid it. She also understood why they'd tried. The closer you got to the granite, the more menacing it appeared.

And now, after walking for an hour, she sat in its damp shadow, close enough to touch. How would she ever climb this monster?

'*Dear Diary*,' wrote Pilgrim, '*what am I going to do?*'

And then the good news, dressed in surprising clothes: a small hole in the rock. Here was a narrow entrance, a doorway leading inside. So Pilgrim's path continued, not over the mountain but through it.

'I'm so glad I don't have to climb,' thought Pilgrim cheerily.

But good news, happily received, can soon lose its shine, and so it was now. She was delighted to be spared the frightening heights. But what awaited her inside this beast? Would the inner path lead Pilgrim to light at the other end? Or would it become a dark labyrinth from which she'd never escape? Good news and bad news are not so different and Pilgrim felt perplexed.

'Dear Diary, in a way, no progress since last entry. I still don't know what to do.'

She looked around for Pointy, last seen dancing in the sunflower field. This would have been a good moment for one of his stones, offering direction. Or Billie the Butterfly perhaps? Where was she when you needed a guide? Nowhere! They were there in the good times but when the chips were down? Even Veronica would have been better than nothing. Just.

'Typical,' said Pilgrim under her breath.

'You called?'

Pilgrim jumped. She'd imagined herself alone but in the dank gloom to her left she could just make out a figure.

'It's enough to make you weep,' said the shape.

'What is?' said Pilgrim.

'This whole mess.'

'What whole mess?

'You! This! What else?'

'Oh I see.'

Pilgrim pondered her disconcerting predicament.

'Here you are, stuck in this God-forsaken place without a clue what to do and no one lifting a finger to help!'

'I suppose so.'

Pilgrim couldn't deny it.

'And it's not the first time you've been let down.'

'That's also true,' said Pilgrim.

She was warming to her new friend who seemed to understand her.

'I've been let down quite a lot,' she added.

This was something long felt by Pilgrim but never spoken. It was good to speak it now.

'Exactly,' said her friend. 'It happens all the time, Pippa. Just when you deserve a break, something always goes wrong.'

'It's the story of my life!'

'Indeed it is. But then what can you expect? You trust people to deliver the goods and what do they do? They let you down with a capital "D".'

'It can be disappointing,' said Pilgrim, feeling a tear coming to her eyes.

'Disappointing? I'd call it infuriating?'

'Infuriating! Yes, it is!' said Pilgrim, glad to name it. 'I could have done so much if I'd been given a break!'

She was suddenly rigid with rage.

'A curse on all who've let you down, Pippa!' said the mist figure.

'That's right!' said Pilgrim. 'A curse on them all, because I don't deserve this, I really don't! Do they know who I am?'

It was at this point that Pilgrim noticed something: she was sinking into the sand. And she noticed something else. The slide had started when she'd got into conversation with old bitter boots in the mist. It was a serious matter for she was now almost down to her waist.

'Help!' she cried out, full of fear. 'Help me out of the sand!'

'Here we go again,' said bitter boots. 'You try and do something good, Pippa, you set out on a journey to heaven and what happens? You begin to sink in the sand and no one comes to help. Typical!'

'I don't need you to tell me how bad it is,' said Pilgrim, 'I need you to help me!'

'I can't help you.'

'But I'm sinking!'

'Of course you're sinking. Story of your life, my girl, but does anyone care?'

'Who are you?

'Tell them they can all go to hell. Tell heaven to go to hell!'

Whoever this was, they gave hopelessness a bad name and Pilgrim wanted shot of them.

'Get lost, whoever you are!' she said.

Pilgrim was slipping further into the cold sand but didn't care any more. All she wanted was to be rid of this man.

'No one tells Self-Pity to get lost!' he said.

'There's a first time for everything.'

'I've got my pride!'

'I know you have. And I've got a rock in my hand with your wretched name on it. Self-Pity, eh? I should have known.'

'I'm the only one who understands you, Pippa! You must see that, after all your pain.'

As Self-Pity hesitated, Pilgrim flung a particularly sharp stone towards him.

'You'll regret this,' he squealed before fading away into the fog.

But Pilgrim didn't regret it for as soon as the figure was gone, her sinking ceased. And now she saw the sign warning travellers about the Sands of Self-Pity. It was not the most visible marker, small, faded and so low in the ground that it was best suited to the pixie community. Little wonder she hadn't seen it; travellers must miss it all the time. Slowly she pulled herself out from the sands and found solid ground once again.

'Phew!' she said

'*Perhaps it's now time to stoop low and enter the* Rock of Hidden Self*,*' she wrote in her diary. '*I'm scared because* I *fear what* I *might find there. Hasn't it all been hidden for a reason?* I *imagine so. But there's so much bottled up inside me* I *feel one day it may choke me completely. So is it really a choice? Perhaps it's time to open the unopened letter.*'

She pondered the small hole in the side of the rock, a rough-hewn door of mystery. She was hesitating and unsure when she heard a voice.

'You look to be in some kind of trouble.'

Pilgrim turned round to see a man of distinctive appearance. He was wearing, from top down, a white trilby hat, a black shirt and black jacket with a white tie, black trousers and white shoes.

'You're completely black and white,' said Pilgrim, unable to hold back from stating the obvious. 'And no shades in between.'

'Just as our good Lord wants it,' said the man.

He also held a large book in his hand, which he waved like a weapon though it turned out to be the Bible, which isn't a weapon at all.

'From where I'm standing you look like a lost soul in need of help,' he said.

For Pilgrim, help was always welcome and especially now as she faced the dark innards of this frightening edifice.

'That's true,' said Pilgrim. 'I need a lot of help right now.'

'Then let me introduce myself. My name's Shaw.'

'Hello Shaw.'

'Shaw Thynge.'

'And my name's Pippa.'

She waited for a reply but none came.

'Pippa Pilgrim.'

There was another silence.

'To be brutally honest, lady,' said Shaw, 'I don't need to know your name.'

'Really?' said Pilgrim. 'The use of names is generally considered polite.'

'God fodder is God fodder, my girl.'

'I accept neither of those descriptions. I am neither fodder nor your girl.'

Shaw Thynge stuck his hands deep into his pockets; perhaps a little too deep.

'Relationship is not important,' he said. 'Are you saved?'

'Er …'

'I thought not.'

'But I do have questions.'

'Questions are to be encouraged, of course.'

'Good!'

Pilgrim was glad to hear this.

'So my first question,' said Pilgrim, but before she could pose it, Shaw Thynge was giving the answer.

'The Shaw Thynge gospel!' he declared.

'Sorry?' said Pilgrim, a little put out.

'I'm just giving you the answer to your question.'

'But I haven't asked it yet.'

'I know, but this way saves time.'

'But how can you answer a question I haven't asked?

'Because whatever the question, the Shaw Thynge gospel is always the answer. Now excuse me a moment.'

'Where are you going?'

Pilgrim watched as the black and white man climbed up onto a nearby rock.

'Ah, that's better!'

'Why have you climbed up there?' asked Pilgrim.

'I prefer a pulpit from which to deliver the truth.'

He seemed happier elevated above normal life.

'But we were having a conversation.'

The man laughed and shook his head in a condescending fashion.

'The truth isn't a dialogue, young Miss. The truth is a

monologue, a monologue from God.'

'Really?' said Pilgrim, looking around with fresh interest. 'Is God on his way?'

'I speak on his behalf.'

'Like many lunatics.'

It just slipped out.

'I need to put you straight on a few matters', said Shaw Thynge firmly, looking down from his pulpit of rock. 'I can do it better from up here.'

Almost vertically above her, looking up at him was uncomfortable, which made Shaw Thynge a real pain in the neck.

'OK,' she said. 'But tell me this: how can you put me straight on a few matters if don't know me?'

'I don't need to know you!'

'Is that so?'

'I just tell people how things are.'

'I see. So how are things?' asked Pilgrim.

'For you?'

'For me.'

'Not good.'

'There's a thing.'

'You're on your way to hell.'

'I see.'

'Eternal damnation.'

'Nothing brief, then?'

'The unquenchable fires, endlessly stoked by demons and accompanied by the gnashing of teeth.'

'Demons as well as gnashing teeth?' said Pilgrim thoughtfully. 'And there was me thinking I was on my way to heaven!'

'Satanic delusion,' said Shaw. 'Take a leaflet.'

Pilgrim hadn't noticed the leaflets available by the rock entrance, entitled 'Avoid Hell Now By Doing What I Tell You'.

'I'll certainly read it.'

'The 27 steps to salvation. It's all pretty straight forward.'

'Will it help me to discover more about the mystery who is me?'

Shaw let out a loud laugh of superiority.

'Lordy Lord! What a god-forsaken notion!'

'I thought it a rather good one; one of my best, in fact.'

'And why, pray, do you need to know anything about yourself?

'Well – '

'You just need to know the loving God. '

'The loving God who's consigning me to hell?'

'Indeed!'

He discerned no fracture in his logic.

'But tell me, Shaw, how can I know anyone, let alone God – who, let's be honest, is a bit mysterious at the best of times – if I don't know myself?'

Shaw Thynge threw his hands in the air in despair.

'Right, that's it! I wipe the dust off my feet!'

'It's sand,' says Pilgrim.

'I'm being metaphorical.'

'Is that good or bad?'

'It means I'm giving up on you.'

'Oh thank you!'

Sometimes it was a huge relief when people gave up on Pilgrim, and so it was now.

'I will leave you to the wicked devices and desires of your heart,' he said, making Pilgrim's life seem a lot more exciting than it was.

Shaw Thynge then came down from his pulpit and gathered up the leaflets from the entrance. A question popped into Pilgrim's mind and she just had to ask:

'Are you happy, Shaw Thynge?'

'Of course I'm happy,' he replied abruptly.

'You hide it well.'

'God's happiness is deep.'

'It must be very deep; invisible from the surface, that's for sure.'

'Enjoy hell,' he said.

And with those encouraging words he was gone and Pilgrim stooped low to enter the dark corridors of the Rock of Hidden Self.

The tenth stage

Pilgrim stood in darkness, unseeing and unknowing. Life had stopped and she knew only disablement and paralysis. The small entrance had offered a little light. But a few steps further into the emptiness had taken her round a corner and into blinding black. This was another world, a world of absence in which she could see nothing, sense nothing and where her skill set (they loved that phrase at work) was reduced to naught.

'*I'm in a place* I *don't know and with no light to guide,*' she wrote in her diary, feeling the pen onto the page. The lines were not straight but had the ring of truth. '*We live the rat-runs of our lives until one day we leave them. I've certainly left mine and – agghh! – a drop of cold water has just hit the back of my neck. Well, I hope it's water.*'

Pilgrim felt panic rise in her and then subside. Here was a sunless place, a moonless and starless cavern, an old and ancient setting and as black as a mine at midnight. But it was also a place she'd been brought to; it was to this place the path had led and she was to trust the path.

'B*ut what of the path when the dark's so deep?*' she wrote.

She started to walk, hands held out before her, feeling her lightless way. And the clues were there, for as she learned from damp touch on cold rock, she was in a tunnel of some sort. And then slowly, as night vision came to her aid, the dark-adapted eye saw further shape in the surrounds. Yes, it was a tunnel, but not an exclusive way, for inside this mountain were a whole series of passages and interconnecting corridors. Maybe an experienced guide could walk them all with her and explain their formation over the years; but Pilgrim had no guide. So she simply walked.

Time passed but beyond the reach of clock and watch, Pilgrim knew only now. She'd rarely felt more alive or more uncertain. Each step took her further from a known way back, from the rough rock door that could return her to the desert light.

'*But you can't turn back and if you try you fail,*' she wrote with difficulty.

The chill had crept slyly upon her and was now paralysing her hands. She desperately needed to find warmth in the cold heart of this mountain. And it was then that Pilgrim saw a hazy light ahead. The source of this glow was hard to discern for it was neither torch nor lantern. Was there perhaps an air hole in the rock reaching up from this place to sky above? But all such wondering stopped when into the light sudden colour appeared and Pilgrim's heart was a-leap. She knew well the one who wore those clothes and there was no person she'd prefer to meet right now.

'Happy!' she shouted out, for who else could the clown be?

Silence.

Pilgrim walked towards the glow and it was as she'd first imagined. The rock had a skylight, a small vertical tunnel, no more than three feet in width, through which the bright moon now shone.

'Happy!' shouted Pilgrim again, her impatience echoing down a thousand stone corridors.

Again silence. Had she been mistaken? And then a footstep on the wet stone. Happy's face appeared from one of the passages, peering disbelief in the half-light.

'Pilgrim?'

'Happy!'

'Pilgrim!'

They rushed towards each other and hugged in the cold.

'So how are you?' asked Pilgrim.

'Never been better!' said Happy.

'Really?'

There was a pause.

'No, not really.'

'Oh.'

'I just got the shock of my life back there.'

'What happened?'

'I can't talk about it now, but it was all a bit unexpected.'

'So why say you're fine when you're not fine?'

'Habit I suppose: "Laugh and the world laughs with you cry and you cry alone."'

'Well, you're not alone now.'

'It's good to see you, Pilgrim.'

'And you, Happy. I can't tell you what a relief it was to see you cross my path. I couldn't believe it.'

They gazed on each other for a moment. And then Happy sighed.

'The journey to heaven is not quite the diamond staircase I imagined,' he said.

'Tell me about it; some of the people I've met!'

Pilgrim wanted to recount amusing stories from her travels with herself cast as the hero. There was the egg-man Breathless and Terrified, the odd and dancing Pointy and the prophet Move-On welded to her stone. Where to begin? But something in Happy's face suggested this wasn't the time for anecdote and laughter.

'You look a little troubled,' she said.

'I am a little troubled.'

'That's OK, we can travel together now. We probably should have done that from the start. I mean, did you meet Self-Pity and Shaw Thynge?'

'Who?'

'It doesn't matter.'

Pilgrim was upset they'd come by different roads to this place. She'd liked to have shared stories.

'And our different paths must continue,' said Happy firmly.

'I don't see why.'

'We cannot travel together.'

'I just feel I should know you better. We're sharing the same journey! That must mean something.'

'It does mean something, and who knows what the future holds. But your way is not mine and I must go now.'

'Well, I'm coming with you for a while. Definitely. And I won't take "No" for an answer. You haven't told me what gave you such a shock back there!'

'Another time.'

'No, this time.'

She couldn't lose Happy now. He was mistaken, surely? She needed him but knew he was gone as he held her shoulders and looked deep into her eyes.

'I love you too much, Pilgrim, to distract you from your path.'

'You wouldn't be distracting me. We'd be a team!'

'Goodbye, Pilgrim, until we meet again.'

With that, he kissed her on the cheek and disappeared down the passage he'd emerged from.

'Come back!' yelled Pilgrim.

She started to chase after him when an extraordinary noise and commotion stopped her. How to describe it? The sound of beating against the rock; a flustered and flapping force in an awkward space. And after a whirlwind of feathers and the scraping of claws on stone, the giant eagle was before her, barring her way. It must have come down the vertical tunnel, battered in passage but now settled menacingly on a ledge

Pilgrim had never trusted this creature and did not start now. The bird was powerful and cruel and most frightening were the eyes which were comprehension; complete comprehension of all things. The animal seemed to see through and beyond her and Pilgrim was unsettled. She didn't want anyone seeing through and beyond her; she wanted Happy laughing by her side.

And the question which could not be ignored: why had the eagle come? Why had it risked such dangerous descent? Pilgrim dreaded to think. This bird of prey would wait its moment and kill in an instant. Pilgrim contemplated the balance of power. Perhaps if she had a spade or blade she could lunge and hurt. Maybe she should throw a rock? Or should she just run? Meanwhile, Pilgrim noticed again the shining gold pendant around the bird's neck, perhaps an identity tag.

'Even assassins have a number,' she thought in the gloom.

And then, what was this? A door opening in the rock! Pilgrim heard it before she saw it. There was a door opening in the rock face and a figure in a shawl stepping out. It was a woman, emerging calmly from the mountain. She glanced briefly around, taking in the bird as if its presence here was nothing unusual. She then turned towards Pilgrim, who sank back into the darkness as best she could. Was this woman the assassin's assistant? Pilgrim was cold, lonely and spent. If the shawl lady carried a stiletto, it would be an easy kill.

'Hello, my beautiful girl,' said the woman with a smile. 'Not tip-top, are you?'

'I am rather cold,' said Pilgrim.

'And from your overall demeanour, I should say your spirit is weary and your genius struggling a little.'

She had Pilgrim's attention. No one had ever spoken of her genius before; indeed no one had spoken in this tone to her before.

'I have felt better,' said Pilgrim, not wishing to sound too well. This attention was not unpleasant.

'Then lie down a moment and let's check you over.'

The woman removed her shawl and placed it under Pilgrim's head for a pillow.

'And who are you?' asked Pilgrim, not wishing to be misled again.

The woman was kneeling by her side, taking her pulse with a nurse's watch on her breast.

'A nurse, really, a nurse of tangled souls,' she said, 'and all seems to be in order. You're in fine physical fettle. So do you fancy a short journey?'

Pilgrim did not fancy a short journey; she'd had enough of journeying, possibly for a lifetime. But then again, these felt like safe hands.

'I should be OK if it's not too demanding,' said Pilgrim with studied weakness.

'Good,' said the nurse, 'because there's something I want you to see.'

Pilgrim was wondering what there could be to see here when she remembered the company she kept.

'I'm not going anywhere while that bird is here,' said Pilgrim.

Whatever it was around the eagle's neck, it glinted even down here.

'You needn't worry about the bird,' said the nurse, packing up her things. 'He was just going anyway.'

And at that moment the eagle launched itself forward, struggling into the air, beating its wings in difficult ascent, spiralling and battering its way out of view towards the night sky.

'Good riddance,' thought Pilgrim.

Nurse helped her to her feet.

'Follow me,' she said and walked back towards the door in the rock from where she'd first appeared.

The nurse had left a lantern in the doorway which she now collected. They then started a long winding descent, down into the bowels of the mountain, via some small but irregular steps. By the time Pilgrim had counted 198 they were deep inside the belly of the rock and standing in a small hallway. The woman with the lamp paused long enough to reveal the signs on one of the doors which said 'Library'. Pilgrim, a keen supporter of her local library, thought this an odd place to find one and said so.

'I can't imagine a great demand for books down here,' she said.

'It's not really that kind of library,' said the nurse.

'What other kind of library is there?' asked Pilgrim.

Another door was opened and Pilgrim was shown into a little room of instant warmth. It was a simple space, clean and fresh with proportions that made her cry as good space can. She wept because this room was kindness and nurse sat with her on the sofa until her sobbing subsided.

'Nothing dries sooner than a tear,' she said.

'No,' said Pilgrim smiling through the rain. 'I don't know what all that nonsense was about!'

'You will,' said nurse. 'But for now, you must make yourself at home. There's tea, coffee or hot chocolate if you like. And cold drinks in the fridge. Orange, apple and mango, cranberry, you know what you like, and biscuits in the tin and some sandwiches, crisps and fruit cake on the side. Take what you want. You must be shattered and starving after all you've been through.'

'It's not quite what I expected when I slipped on the stairs this morning! Or whenever it was.'

'No, it will all have been a shock.'

They sat quietly for a while.

'Life is sometimes fired at point-blank range,' said the nurse gently. 'But what a star you've been.'

'Oh, I wouldn't say that!'

Pilgrim was not comfortable with praise.

'Really? Why ever not?'

'Well, I – '

'I've watched in amazement, to be honest, and you're definitely my Best Girl today, Pilgrim.'

Pilgrim's face flushed with pleasure.

'Best Girl? I wish you'd tell my mother.'

'I don't need to, Pilgrim. I'm telling you. You're the only one who need know.'

'I suppose.'

Pilgrim remembered Happy's unfortunate experience of being defined by another. But she too had allowed it, always a beggar for the good opinion of those around. So nurse's words felt both new and strange.

'So what's, er, so good about me?' asked Pilgrim.

'That's not the real question.'

'It isn't?'

'No.'

'So what's the real question?'

'The real question is this: what is it that destroyed the sense of your own wonder?'

Pilgrim suddenly groaned and pushed forward. Some dam was opened inside and impelled by her body and forces unknown, she found herself thrown to the floor. Sealed pain was unsealed and a terrible energy released, twisting her body, stretching out her arms. Sometimes she'd push nurse away, pummelling her with blows; and sometimes she'd reach out, grab nurse's hand and place it on her burning back for respite and for touch. Nurse would draw her hand slowly down Pilgrim's arching spine, bringing rest and relief, a brief lull, before contortions resumed, driven from within, shoulders rolling, arms stretching in writhing expurgation of far-in-the-past things.

Nurse stayed close until exhaustion set in. She helped a dazed Pilgrim back to her seat, offering a shoulder as pillow for her head.

They sat in silence for a while before Pilgrim spoke:

'I'm worried,' said Pilgrim, as the years fell away from her soul. 'I'm worried about everything.'

And then quietly, nurse spoke:

'You neither worry from morning to evening, nor from evening to morning. Do not concern yourself with things which might or might not be, for you are more brilliant than the morning and wiser than the evening. That is how things are, sweet Pilgrim. We shall recover your soul.'

'It can get lost along the way.'

'Mislaid, perhaps.'

Pilgrim had enjoyed a hot bath and refreshing sleep when nurse returned.

'I've got to be off now, Best Girl, but we'll meet again.'

'I hope so.'

'I know so. But I can't come with you.'

'That's what Happy said.'

'He was right, there's a season for everything. And sometimes you're stronger alone.'

'Maybe. I mean, in a way, I don't mind what experiences I have, just so long as I feel better, feel more secure.'

There was a pause. Nurse sat herself on the edge of the chair and spoke with deliberation:

'Pilgrim, I know it's hard, but do this one thing.'

'What's that?'

'Release each experience from the obligation of making you feel better or more secure. Can you do that?'

'Of course not! And why would I even want to?'

'Why?'

'Yes, why?'

Nurse paused like one entrusted with difficult things, with mysteries beyond telling.

'Beyond feeling better and secure, Pilgrim, states which are sometimes just cheap anaesthetics, is feeling true, being true, being true to who you are rather than to some makeshift and deluded self-image. I want you to be free, Pilgrim, and being free is allowing every experience to speak and every feeling to speak, not just those that dull the pain. No turning away!'

Pilgrim could see how free that would be; though like heaven, it seemed a faraway thing right now.

'And don't underestimate your power, Pilgrim,' continued nurse as she picked up her coat.

'Power? What power do I possess?'

This was another new idea.

'I don't have any power,' continued Pilgrim. 'Others have power, but not me. Half the time I don't even feel like I exist!'

'There you go again, Pilgrim, belittling yourself.'

'So what power do I have?'

'The power of your heart, sweet girl, what else?'

'The power of my heart?'

'The power of your heart. Now when you're ready, the door is over there.'

'Which door?'

'The door to the library.'

Pilgrim looked up. She hadn't noticed the entrance but like a hungry dog it stared at her now.

'You never told me your name,' said Pilgrim.

'My name is Grace.'

'I don't deserve you.'

'Oh you do, Pilgrim, you do. More than words can say.'

'Will you help me get to heaven?'

Grace's smile was like sunlight in a cell.

'Til soon,' she said.

Pilgrim sat pondering the door. She'd enjoyed her moment of Grace but noticed a change now.

'*I'm feeling unsettled and* I *don't know why*,' she wrote, as she drank tea and finished off the flapjack. 'I *felt safe with Grace around but* I *think the door is making me nervous. Why,* I *have no idea. What is there to fear in a library, for goodness sake? It's not as if I've some overdue books to declare.'*

Pilgrim put her diary down for a moment, before deciding on one more entry: '*Grace may be right about there being a season for everything but I wish there wasn't. What's wrong with just wanting to feel better? I wish I could get to heaven on a magic carpet flying high above reality.*'

Pilgrim returned the diary to her pocket, stood up and started to walk. Sometimes you cross a room and think nothing of it. At other times, each step counts and this was so as Pilgrim neared the door. It was an old wooden door, cobalt blue, paint slightly peeling and hinges rusty with neglect. There was also an old brass plaque offering the following instructions:

> Dear User,
>
> If at any time you need assistance in the library, please do not ask the staff. There are none.
>
> Seek in yourself for what you need and out of compassion for your self will come insight, strength and healing.
>
> Do not ask the staff for such things because there are none available today. Or ever.

Pilgrim took a deep breath and turned the large key. It complained, jammed, but then clicked free: the library door was unlocked. Pilgrim lifted the latch, pulled the door open and stepped inside.

The eleventh stage

The library is large, high-ceilinged like a stately home and silent as a church.The stillness is solid and Pilgrim knows instantly where she is. There are countless old statues and portraits but, above all else, there are books and then more books, some on the high, heaving shelves, others in piles on the floor, waiting to be sorted. And every statue, every portrait and every book she touches with her shaking hands is about Pilgrim, about Pippa from womb until now. Here is everything noted, everything stored, everything recorded in intimate and honest detail.

Pilgrim is fighting for breath, aware of the dangerous treasure in her grasp, when she hears a noise. Looking up, she sees movement at the other end of the room, something knocked over, a figure in the shadows. The shocking realisation: she is not alone in the library. Someone else is here as well. But who can it be?

Pilgrim stands still, her heart beating hard and fast. And then there's the figure again, closer now, perceived through the half-light and a separating shelf of books.

'Not you!' exclaims Pilgrim.

In that instant, she decides to run. Where to, she doesn't know but sometimes terror is its own direction. Seeking escape, she runs past one pile of books, then another, flees down one aisle, up another, turns a corner and then – aaggh!

What is this before her? If frightened before, she could now hardly move for shock:

'No one should have to see this!' she gasps, her attention transfixed by the object before her. 'No one should have to see this!'

She should never have come here. Making haste towards the nearest door, she hopes for release above all things, release from this place. But will the door open and will she be let out?

'Yes!' she exclaims, as the door swings back.

She moves quickly and stands now in the hallway she'd passed through with Grace. It's time to be gone. With fear as fuel, she runs up the 198 stairs and through the rock door to the mountain passage where she'd left Happy. Lungs aching, Pilgrim remembers the bird and becomes vigilant again. She fears those talons but, thank God, the creature is gone. Pilgrim begins to relax, a feeling encouraged by the distant light at the end of the tunnel.

'Yes!' she says again, only louder than before.

Could the light really be true? Like a crazed island castaway who, believing they've seen a boat, rushes from jungle to shore, so Pilgrim now makes for the light. With each second and each step the white ball grows. She stumbles the final few yards to the entrance, hands shielding her eyes from the dazzle.

In the sun at last, she stands in the oldest back door in the world, a rock arch smoothed by the passing of a billion years. And beneath her feet, there's writing deep-carved in the stone. Lowering herself to her knees and clearing away obscuring dust, she reads words embedded in the granite of eternity.

> Pause, dear traveller, but do not look back to former times. Remember Lot's wife. Leave behind that which you were, for that which you were is now dead. And remember Lot's wife who was led by the angels out of the city of Sodom, a place of death where they could no longer live. The angels led them to the great plain of freedom.
>
> You would not stand where you stand, traveller or survey that which you survey unless you too seek freedom. Your world is created by your disposition and your disposition is for freedom; but your training is in slavery.
>
> So remember Lot's wife and the psychological meaning. Like a dog returning to its vomit, she lingered in former ways, looking back on old times and former states. Thus she became something dead, a pillar of salt, unable to leave what she was, unable to become what she might be.
>
> Do not cling to the Sodom of Ignorance but let the seed of esoteric knowledge grow within, for as it grows, you grow. Make for the chasm you cannot cross and remembering Lot's wife, do not look back.

Pilgrim wished she knew more about Lot's wife. She also wondered why anyone would waste their time making for a chasm no one could cross. But such thoughts were dispensed with as a figure approached her across the plain. He was doing cartwheels and pirouettes, which made him distinctive in the dry air. The red braces and baggy trousers were the final clue.

'Pointy!'

'Ah, if it isn't Pilgrim!'

He seemed a little flustered as she climbed down the rock to greet him.

'What are you doing here?' she asked.

'I'm not here for you, I'm afraid.'

'Charming!' said Pilgrim.

'Just speaking the truth,' he said. '"Keeping it real", as they say.'

Keeping it real? Where did he find his phrases? Was there a youth club nearby?

'So tell me, Pointy: where are you going?'

'I'm on my way to help someone else. So for me as a guide, you're unpaid and therefore unwanted overtime.'

'You're doing wonders for my self-esteem.'

'I'm just saying.'

'But can't you help me a bit, Pointy?'

'Not really, no.'

'Oh.'

Pilgrim was feeling crushed when suddenly Pointy's face lit up.

'But you can help me!' he said.

'How?'

Pointy removed his spectacles with fresh intent.

'It's good that we've bumped into each other, Pilgrim.'

'That's a change of heart.'

'No, it's really very good.'

'Because?'

'How can I put this?'

'Just get to the point.'

'I need you to wear my spectacles.'

'And why would I do that?'

'Just do it,' said Pointy and, like a doormat, she did as she was told. She placed Pointy's spectacles on her nose after which he drew a comb from his back pocket, like a musketeer unsheathing his sword, and in the glass reflection of his spectacles attended to his hair with both concern and precision.

The grooming process took awhile, and with each passing moment Pilgrim became more and more irritated at her compliance in this vain charade.

'I've never seen such busy combing by one with so little hair,' she mused.

It should be said that Pointy was entirely bald but for one long and determined strand.

'Would tweezers be a better option?' continued Pilgrim.

No response.

'I mean, you are quite literally combing your "hair".'

Pilgrim felt pleased. She'd turned the tables rather well and it was good to have the last laugh.

'How was the library?' asked Pointy, as he sheathed his comb and took his glasses back.

The last laugh turned to dust in Pilgrim's mouth.

'The library?'

The words came out disastrously high.

'You have a grand spirit, my girl, but this isn't a competition. I just sensed something went wrong.'

'Nothing went wrong in the library. Why would you think something went wrong?'

Pointy sighed.

'Just make for the chasm, Pilgrim.'

The chasm? This was not a good time to mention the chasm.

'This wouldn't by any chance be the chasm you cannot cross?' she said sneeringly. 'I hear about this chasm as something really important, yet you cannot cross it! So I'm standing here asking myself: what's the point? What's the point of making for a chasm you cannot cross?'

Pointy was dancing again, taking Pilgrim with him, but they ended their sequence with his face, and particularly his nose, very close and adjacent. She might have felt intimidated by a man's face so close but for Pointy's surprisingly fresh breath, mint with a trace of eucalyptus.

'You speak correctly,' said Pointy, 'but not wisely. You cannot cross the chasm; but that doesn't mean the chasm cannot be crossed.'

'How so?'

'The statements are both true in their way but one is more true than the other. You understand?'

'No.'

'There are degrees of truth, Pilgrim.'

'I don't agree. Either something is true or it isn't.'

'Wait a minute.'

'Where are you going?'

Pointy returned with a long pole found by the side of the road. Had a circus passed this way?

'See this?' said Pointy, laying the pole on the ground in front of her.

'Yes.'

'If truth is black and this end' – he points to the left – 'and false is white and this end' – he points to the right – 'then in between are a lot of shades of grey, getting darker as they near the truthful black and paler as they near the false white. You follow so far?'

'I think so.'

'So two statements can be true in their way but one might be truer than the other.'

'You mean they both might be grey but one might be a darker grey.'

'Precisely!' said Pointy.

'So very few things are utterly, always and completely true, just as very few things are utterly, always and completely false?'

'You're a good pupil, Pilgrim,' said Pointy with some pride. 'Most statements are a shade of grey. And it's up to you to spot whether it's a light grey or a dark grey.'

'We need the gift of discernment,' said a reflective Pilgrim.

'We do indeed. But that's enough unpaid overtime. You must pay attention, my girl, and good luck!'

And with that he swung away and was gone, gliding his way into the distance like a loose-trousered goblin – with one hair.

Pilgrim stood alone in the desert. She was grateful for Pointy's linguistic analysis and stimulated by it.

'*It's just like being a student again!*' she wrote excitedly in her diary, alongside her extensive 'grey pole of truth' notes.

But beyond the thrill and buzz of the lecture room was the feeling of being alone again. She met people whom she hoped would help, but they were like the grass, here today, gone tomorrow. She wanted to see Grace again but what would she say? How could she ever face her after what happened in the library? Pilgrim did feel very alone.

She surveyed the horizon but there was nothing to see except a stone plinth. A stone plinth! How hadn't she noticed it? It wasn't large but neither was it small, and the question was this: could it have been left there by Pointy? Closer inspection suggested yes, for on the top of the plinth was Pointy's trademark sharpened stone, clearly directing her to the left over the ridge. More intriguing still were the two words inscribed on the stone, inexpertly chiselled:

Ah! Talk of heaven at last! When signposts acknowledge your destination, it's a clue you're getting close, and the thought that she was nearing the Promised Land gave fresh impetus for her journey.

She checked the angle of the stone against the position of the sun, licked her finger and held it in the air, because that's what you do, and then put her best foot forward. Pilgrim had definitely turned a corner.

'To heaven!' she exclaimed in dramatic tones given that no one was listening.

'To heaven!' shouted Veronica, giving Pilgrim a terrible shock.

Where had the rat appeared from? She was sitting on a stone scratching a dumbo ear with her back leg.

'Oh, it's you,' said Pilgrim looking down at the vermin in every possible way. Pilgrim wanted company, but company of her choosing, company to make her feel good. Grace was a friend, Veronica an acquaintance. Was it a crime to think in this way?

They'd last met in the Garden of Sadness, which seemed so long ago.

'It was a time of great happiness,' thought Pilgrim, 'but in a way, so what?'

The happiness hadn't lasted and, after all she'd been through, Pilgrim wanted a bit of fun, some happy distraction and Veronica here was hardly the Queen of Party.

'You're doing well, Pilgrim,' she said.

'I know I'm doing well,' said Pilgrim. 'I don't need you to tell me.'

'Good.'

'And I'm doing it despite the attentions of that hateful eagle.'

Pilgrim was once again aware of its circling presence.

'The thing is, Pilgrim, and you mustn't take this amiss – '

'Believe me, Ratty, there's nothing you can say that will even remotely disturb my peace of mind.'

'That's good, because you mustn't punish yourself about the library incident.'

'Oh, for goodness sake!' thought Pilgrim furiously. 'Someone else bringing up the library incident! What's the big deal? So things happened in the library – get over it, all of you! Why can't you all just keep your noses out of my business?'

'I'm not punishing myself about the library incident,' said Pilgrim tersely.

'Shame can do terrible things to us.'

'And your point is?'

'Well, to escape the hell of our shame we tend to transfer it on to others. It's a lesson from history.'

'I don't care!'

Veronica paused and shook her head slowly.

'Never happy words those.'

'Really? Well, I don't care again!'

'"I don't care", Pilgrim, are the words of those running from unresolved things.'

'I don't care! I don't care! I don't care!'

'Frightened, closed-up words.'

'And I still don't care! The past is the past, Ratty! Just move on! Chill out! I'm on my way to heaven. And do you know what? I'll get there without you!'

The twelfth stage

Pilgrim and her huff strode off into the desert. It was a decisive statement of independence and separation; Pilgrim felt the last laugh was definitely hers.

'I *do enjoy having the last laugh*,' she scribbled as she walked furiously on. '*Particularly over Veronica!*'

But soon a problem became apparent: Pilgrim couldn't remember which ridge to aim for. Pointy's stone had been very clear but now she couldn't be sure and going back to check was not an option. She might meet Veronica again, which would be awkward.

'If you slam the front door behind you and declare "That's it! We're through!" you can't then return two minutes later to collect your hat.'

Pilgrim was lost. In the absence of other aids, she looked to the sky for clues but more for effect than help. No matter how many times you've seen Lawrence of Arabia, and Pilgrim had sat through it more than once with her dad, the sun is an inaccurate guide to the untutored eye.

As it turned out, however, she needn't have worried. On reaching the top of the first ridge she was looking down on heaven or something very like it. Here was a gleaming city teeming with life. Indeed, she'd hardly taken two steps towards it when she was caught in a crowd which, like a great wave, swept her towards the city centre. She found herself walking next to a young woman.

'Is this heaven?' asked Pilgrim.

'Pretty much,' said the young woman.

'How can it be "pretty much" heaven?'

'It's the City of Socialmeja stupid. Keep up!'

'Oh, I see!' said Pilgrim hastily.

She did not want to be perceived as one not keeping up.

'And your name?' asked Pilgrim of her new companion.

'Dee.'

'Dee?'

'Dee Straction.'

'Lovely name and just who I've been looking for. My name's Pilgrim.'

'Pilgrim?'

'Yep.'

'Mor-bid!'

'Is it? said Pilgrim.

'Totally.'

Like a weak captain on a sinking ship, Pilgrim decided on hasty abandonment of her identity.

'It's not my real name, of course.'

'It isn't?

'No way! My real name's Pippa.'

'Better.'

'I was just joking about Pilgrim.'

'You're a strange one.'

'It's a ridiculous name.'

'You're not wrong there!

Relieved to have escaped embarrassment, Pilgrim now wished to hear all about her new home.

'So tell me what's so heavenly about the City of Socialmeja?'

'It's where we're all, like, connected with every one and every thing!'

'Wow!' said Pilgrim for the first time in her life. Wow? Where did that come from? Why was she trying to be all young again? 'Yes, I can see that's pretty heavenly!'

'So I'm talking to you, sure,' said Dee, 'total attention and all that, but I'm also texting a friend, tweeting my whereabouts to my 476 followers, checking my Facebook page, watching a film and trying to rent a house with some friends – all at the same time on this little gizmo!'

Dee waved a small piece of technology at her. Pilgrim marvelled at its smart simplicity and felt thrilled to be part of this really great group of people.

'It's all about connecting,' said Dee.

'It is indeed and you don't know how good it feels to be connecting again.'

'Sorry?'

'I said it's great to be connecting again.'

'Hang on a sec, Pauline –

' – Pippa.'

'Pippa, yeh. I'm just getting a reply to my tweet –

' – Oh I see –

' – and we're approaching a good bit in the film.'

'Oh, right.'

'Ah! Great!'

'Good news?'

'A possible flat to rent! I need to call them.'

'Of course.'

'538 Facebook friends by the way.'

'Really?'

'Tell a lie, 539! A new one. Who can that be? Let's have a look.'

'What about the film?'

'I'm getting back to that in a moment.'

And that was the last Pilgrim saw of Dee Straction because now another crowd surged towards her. Without realising it, Pilgrim had climbed on to a stage where a teenage girl was overcome with excitement.

'I've just won *The Fame Game*!' she exclaimed hysterically. 'Oh my God! I've just won *The Fame Game*!'

The crowd was also hysterical – it seemed a requirement to be here – while cameras flashed and microphones were shoved under her nose.

'Oh, well done!' said Pilgrim, rather caught up in the hysteria. 'That's fantastic!'

'It's been a journey,' said the young woman breathlessly. 'But what a night! What. A. Night!'

Pilgrim thought this an odd remark as the sun was still high in the sky. There was a sense that the winner spoke borrowed words. There was a pre-packaged quality to them.

'I made it through the rain,' she said tearfully, as the crowds were held back by hastily erected barriers. 'I wanted to do it my way, be myself and I was. My public wanted the real me, they got the real me and voted me the winner.'

Cue more hysterical screaming.

'It's just, well, what can I say? It's been a journey. I want to thank all my fans!'

Yet more hysterical screaming, with fainting, and Pilgrim couldn't help but enjoy her obvious delight.

'That's really terrific,' said Pilgrim, who seemed to be her interviewer. 'Er – sorry, I don't know your name.'

'Gullible,' said the young woman. 'Call me Gullible.'

'Well, Gullible, you must tell me what you had to do to win *The Fame Game*!'

Everyone was going mad around her, holding out autograph books like begging bowls. This young woman must have done something pretty remarkable.

'I was five foot three tall,' she said

'I beg your pardon?'

'I was five foot three inches tall.'

'Yes, but what did you do?'

'That's what I did. I was five foot three inches tall.'

'And that was enough?'

'Why certainly!'

'Gullible, Gullible!' chanted the crowd.

'To win *The Fame Game*,' explained Gullible, 'you had to be five foot three inches tall and I was.'

'Was no one else that height?'

'Not like I was. I mean, another girl was five foot two and three-quarter inches; she was the other finalist. But the judges gave her a pretty hard time.'

'They didn't like her not being five foot three?'

'No, they did not! But they thought I was great, they said that I "nailed it". You just have to believe in yourself. It was my time.'

Pilgrim was feeling nauseous.

'I always knew it was in me,' said Gullible.

'But there wasn't anything in you,' said Pilgrim, uncharitably. 'You just happened, quite by chance, to be the right height. That's not virtue, that's luck.'

'Excuse me, but I must intervene,' said a smooth-looking man in shades, as a bouncer shepherded Gullible away from both Pilgrim and the screaming fans. Judging from the increased decibel level, the smooth-looking man was even more popular than Gullible. He acknowledged the adulation with a wave of his well-jewelled hand.

'And you are?' asked Pilgrim.

'Desperate.'

'I'm sorry,' said Pilgrim. 'Have the crowd mistaken you for someone famous?'

'No,' said Desperate firmly. 'I am famous.'

'Oh really?'

'Very famous.'

'I'm happy for you.'

'More famous than you'll ever be. "Desperate" is just my nickname.'

'Ah! And your full name?

'Lee Shallow. "Desperate" Lee Shallow at your socially mobile service.'

'Pippa Pilgrim,' said Pilgrim.

'And this is Blond,' said Shallow.

He pointed to the woman by his side who smiled through bright white teeth.

'And what do you do, Blond?' asked Pilgrim, sounding a little like the queen.

'She's blond,' said Shallow.

'Does she talk for herself?'

'She can talk,' said Shallow, 'does a little TV work, but she's mainly blond. One of the best blonds I've worked with.'

'High praise indeed,' said Pilgrim.

The irony flew way over Shallow's well-groomed head, which then turned to Pilgrim in a conspiratorial manner:

'And tittle-tattle in the press about Blond and I being lovers, is just that, tittle-tattle!'

'I'm sorry?'

Pilgrim was wondering why he was saying this.

'Tittle-tattle in the press about Blond and I being lovers,' he repeated in a louder voice and into a hastily convened microphone, 'Well, my lips are sealed! No brief features, with photos, in the celebrity gossip pages please!'

'You're mistaking me for someone who's interested,' said Pilgrim, who for once in her life was wondering if there was someone more interesting in the room.

Shallow moved fast to re-establish his credentials.

'I'm the genius who fronts *The Fame Game*, by the way, the No. 1 hit TV show. And I also handle the affairs of Gullible.'

Pilgrim pondered this bleak union.

'I could also handle yours,' he added.

'I beg your pardon?'

'Your affairs!'

'Oh I see. You mean I could be as famous as you?'

'Not as famous as me, no, because I'm ultra-famous.'

'Fair point.'

'But you could be partially famous, which is better than not being famous at all.'

'I suppose so.'

'I know so.'

'And remind me: the benefits of fame are?'

With most fame based on a little gift and a lot of luck, Pilgrim sensed only hollowness at the heart of the ideal.

'Are you joking?' said Shallow. 'When you're famous people know who you are.'

'There's a thought.'

'No, there's a gold mine.'

'But I have a problem with that.'

'A problem?'

'Well, how can anyone else know who I am when I don't?'

At that moment there was a disturbance in the crowd and Shallow moved quickly towards the source, a new arrival on the scene.

'And who might you be?' demanded Shallow.

'The space man,' came the reply. 'I tried last year and you turned me away.'

'Oh yes, I remember.'

'I wondered if you'd changed your mind.'

The new arrival was a strong figure, muscled and tough like a ploughman of old. And behind him, he dragged a huge amount of space which he seemed to be offering to the city.

'And what's this you've brought with you?'

'I bring space, if you remember,' said the space man. 'I like to offer it to the busiest of places.'

'Because?'

'Because if busy places lack space they also lack tenderness and hope.'

Shallow raised his eyebrows in comical fashion.

'Tenderness and hope? Are you from another century or something?'

'No, I'm from now. How about you?'

Fear flickered across Shallow's face before charming control was resumed.

'Look, mate, I've got no problems with the idea of space, none at all,' he said, 'but there's absolutely no way we could handle this much.'

He gestured dismissively towards the spaciousness on offer.

'There's just too much going on here,' he continued. 'I can hardly stop all the activity just for a bit of space! Get real!'

'Anxious activity is all the better for space.'

'Who said it was anxious?'

'The eyes are always the giveaway,' said the space man. 'Perhaps that's why you hide yours.'

Shallow's dark glasses stared impassively at the space man.

'How about making the space smaller,' said Shallow, 'much smaller.'

'You can't make space smaller,' said the space man, 'it's eternal.'

Something turned inside Shallow. This was all becoming an irritating waste of time.

'I'm sorry, but this conversation is going nowhere.'

'No, my friend, it's you who's going nowhere.'

'I beg your pardon?'

'That's why I'm here, because you're going nowhere.'

'You rude little oik? Thug! Brutal!'

Two men in red T-shirts quickly moved in.

'Without space,' said the space man, 'there's no tenderness – '

But those were his last words as a fierce fist smashed him to the floor and he was dragged off backstage to be taught a lesson.

'Dispose of the space man,' said Shallow to Thug, Head of Security. 'I don't want him speaking to anyone here. He's dangerous.'

'Consider him dead, sir.'

Pilgrim felt sick.

'Now, where were we, Pippa?' said Shallow, as Blond lit a cigarette for him. 'Ah yes, we were about to make you famous.'

Pilgrim left the city of Socialmeja shortly after, much to Shallow's displeasure and amazement.

'Leave this place and you're heading for certain death,' he said.

'Isn't that the condition of us all, Shallow?'

Shallow smiled wearily.

'Maybe, Pippa, but you rather sooner than me!'

'I'm not sure the word "sooner" exists in eternity,' she replied. 'And by the way, it's Pilgrim.'

'Oh to be a pilgrim – not! I'm building my own empire here!'

'No, you're building your own gibbet here. Goodbye, Shallow.'

The thirteenth stage

On leaving the city of Socialmeja, Pilgrim was overwhelmed once again with feelings of resentment towards Veronica and soon found herself in the village of Lower Bile. Tiring of her journey she decided to seek refreshment and, looking up, saw a large inn dominating the High Street.

'That's the place to go,' said a stranger, carrying an awkward load.

He was a rotund figure with a red face framed by various chins. He sweated and wheezed his way to Pilgrim's side.

'You recommend it?' she asked.

'Well, you can see for yourself how popular it is!'

It was certainly a busy establishment.

'As it happens,' he continued, 'I'm going there myself if you want to come along.'

Pilgrim was pleased to hear this. It was good to find a friend in a strange village.

'Why not?' said Pilgrim and without a further thought or a glance at the sign, she followed the stranger to Inn Dignation.

'I'm Ivor, by the way,' said her host as they settled at a table in the corner.

'And I'm Pilgrim.'

'Ivor Grudge.'

'Who hasn't?'

'No, that's my name.'

'Oh, I see. And the load you carry?'

'Need you ask? I have a sack full of grievances and personal slights stored in here.'

It was a large and awkward sack.

'And you won't put down these slights even to eat?'

'What? And let them all off the hook? I won't give them the pleasure!' he said proudly.

'Though it seems you're more on the hook than they are,' ventured Pilgrim.

'Nonsense!' said Grudge.

Pilgrim glanced eagerly at the menu but was not encouraged. Only two drinks were on offer:

Bitter or Whine

And under food, it simply said:

Sour cream

'I'm here to meet my solicitors,' said Grudge. 'They'll be pursuing certain grievances on my behalf. They could act for you as well. It's not a speedy process, of course, it can take years and years to get to court, but it's important we don't put our grievances down.'

'I suppose so,' said Pilgrim, watching Grudge being crushed by his.

'Indeed, let's see my legal fellows now before we eat. Follow me!'

Grudge led a reluctant Pilgrim across the bar. They arrived at a door on which it said:

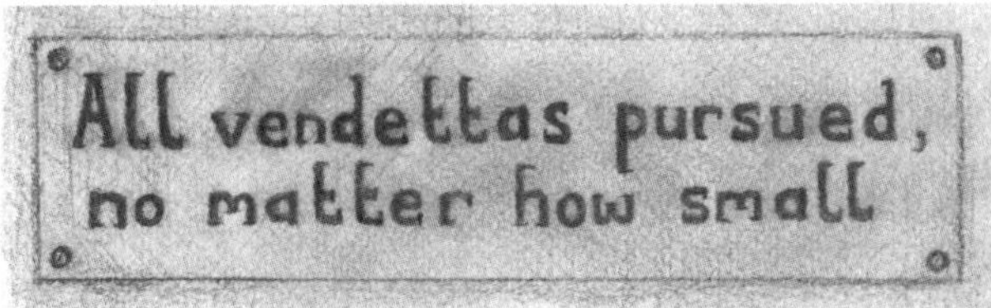

The door opened on to a claustrophobic staircase which led down to the cellar beneath Inn Dignation.

'These are their offices,' said Grudge.

'Whose offices?'

In the musty half-light, three pale individuals sat at a table composing resentful letters and emails.

'Let me introduce you to my solicitors, Huff, Tiff and Bitch.'

One of them coughed in the stale air, releasing odious breath before stuffing some more folders in Grudge's sack.

'More replies and counter-arguments,' said Huff. 'I don't think you'll like them one little bit.'

'These matters, though apparently minor initially, would appear to be growing in rancour,' said Tiff, smiling for the first time.

'Shall we continue to act meanly on your behalf?' said Bitch.

'Oh certainly,' said Grudge, wilting under the new weight of grievance and counter-grievance. 'Certainly!'

Pilgrim had seen enough.

'Ivor, come with me.'

'I'm busy.'

Ignoring his words, Pilgrim grabbed him by the hand and pulled him through the back door into a courtyard.

'There's a strange smell here,' said Grudge nervously.

'Yes, it's called fresh air.'

'I best be getting back.'

'But why, Grudge? We could leave the sack here and find a new path for you!'

'And let them off the hook? Never!'

'Goodbye, Grudge,' said Pilgrim, knowing it was time to leave. 'But when the path finds you, don't be afraid.'

'Path? What path?'

But the fresh air was making Grudge choke and cling ever more firmly to his sack of gall and offence; though where he ended and his sack began was increasingly hard to tell.

And Pilgrim hadn't walked far when another brief encounter occurred.

'Can I walk with you?' said a fellow traveller.

He was a clean-shaven man in a smart uniform. Police? Navy? Air Force? It was hard to be sure but the gold stripes spoke of rank and competence. And not before time you might say!

'By all means,' said Pilgrim, glad of such company.

'You're probably nervous about your journey from here,' he said, clearly used to handling raw recruits.

'A little bit, yes. You never know what's round the corner.'

'And, let's not to beat about the bush, you've taken a few wrong turnings along the way.'

Pilgrim nodded.

'Ignored the navigational beacons, so to speak.' he continued.

'I have, yes.'

'Big mistake.'

He nodded in agreement with his own sagacity.

'Right.'

'Textbook errors obviously.'

'Obviously.'

'Schoolboy stuff.'

'Schoolgirl.'

'Don't try and be clever now!'

'But having established my mistakes,' said Pilgrim hopefully, 'can you now help me with the path ahead?'

'Me?

'Yes.'

'No.'

'No?'

'Take a long, hard look at yourself, Pilgrim! You've made a pretty poor shift of things so far; total cock-up from beginning to end.'

'I'm aware of that,' said Pilgrim, patience at breaking point.

'Choices made which now you regret.'

Pippa felt like crying.

'You're not helping.'

'It's quite clear to me where you went wrong.'

'You don't say?'

'We could undertake a strategic review if you like, look at each scenario in turn. I call them the "dunce moments".'

'The dunce moments?'

'The dunce moments, yes, the daft decisions which with a bit more thought, with a little pre-operational planning, you could have avoided.'

Before committing any further words to the conversation, Pilgrim reflected for a moment.

'Do you have a name?' she asked.

'Eustace Hindsight at your service.'

'Useless Hindsight?'

'Eustace Hindsight.'

'Well, Useless – '

'Eustace – '

'I'm sorry. Now tell me, Eustace, do you do anything other than "obvious"?'

'Post-op de-brief's my thing. They call me the King of Clarity.'

'Only when you're in the room, I suspect.'

It was at this point, Pilgrim realised, they'd reached a dead end in the road.

'You've led me into a cul-de-sac,' said Pilgrim.

'Procedurally speaking – '

' – my biggest dunce moment was giving you the time of day. Goodbye, Useless.'

And so it was that Pilgrim left behind Eustace Hindsight and the village of Lower Bile. And as she walked, she found herself climbing a steep mountain path. Soon she was looking down on the fields below, a patchwork of green and brown squares. As for Inn Dignation, so large in the High Street, it was now tiny.

'*Strange how something that appeared so big,*' she wrote, '*can now appear so small and insignificant.*'

And as she walked on, her lungs rejoiced. Here was a land of clean air, deep snow and tall evergreens soaring into the blue sky. Here was spaciousness for the soul, a silent and healing glory. And such flowers along the way! The pastel yellows of Cold Mountain Crazyweed; the rich orange of Golden Cinquefoil; the gentle purple of Alpine Gentian and the creamy-white beauty of Edelweiss. If heaven was better than this, it must be very good indeed.

But as Pilgrim tried to gather her thoughts, she found they wouldn't stay still. They were like a dust storm in her head, confused and obscuring. What should she be thinking? What to make of Grace, Pointy, Shallow and Grudge? What to make of anything? But nothing came to mind, apart from more questions and more dust clouds.

'*Perhaps,*' she wrote in her diary, in a moment of particular frustration, '*it is best not to think at all but just walk.*'

And this is what she did. Pilgrim walked and walked, enjoying the energy in her body. Her heart beat in happy labour and eventually, with sweat on her brow, her path of solitude through the snowy wood brought her to the Clearing of Stillness. Here there was no sound but creeping moss on the trees and icicle fingers growing. In the middle of the clearing were a wooden table and chair, centuries old, and Pilgrim sat for a while, without purpose or aim. And as she listened to her breathing, sanity returned, something unlocked and she found within her the capacity to face anything that arose.

'I *feel so strong*,' she wrote.

Her breathing brought calm and calm brought space in which doors of sense and feeling opened. And while much passed through her, nothing stayed to oppress. Like small clouds in a huge sky, she watched things come and go, aware of them all but unattached to any.

'On the journey to heaven,' she wrote in her diary, 'I sometimes forget that I'm going to a place where it's better than before. And that I'm going home, that I walk towards a homecoming. So why do I resist? And what do I resist? Amid the beauty I now contemplate, the snow, the flowers and the silence of the soaring trees, I resist nothing.'

She knew she was at peace when she found herself smiling at the eagle high in the mountain sky.

'It's just looking for a homecoming like the rest of us,' she thought.

After a few more happy minutes she was making to leave the clearing when a woman arrived at her side.

'Bills, eh?' she said.

'I beg your pardon?'

'It's nothing but bills, bills and more bills these days.'

Pilgrim was looking at a tall, angular woman who seemed able only to see and move in a very limited way.

'I was just thinking how beautiful it all was,' said Pilgrim.

'And if it's not bills, it's the tax man,' she continued.

'Have you not seen the Gentian?'

Apparently not.

'Bills and taxes! Expense, expense, expense! They get you in the end, one way or another.'

'Who's 'they'?

'The government, business, work, friends, family – everyone!'

'My name's Pilgrim, by the way.'

'And I'm Dismal.'

'You're not wrong there.'

'And I don't think the snow's done much for my shoes, they'll need replacing.'

'Perhaps just some polish – '

'And the way people treat you, eh?'

'Er – '

'They don't know they're born, some people. I was just saying the other day that when I was a girl – '

'Actually, Dismal,' said Pilgrim in a polite but firm manner, 'if it's all the same to you, I'll be moving on.'

'No such thing,' she said. 'It's one step forward, two steps back. Fact.'

'Well – '

'And they should do something about this table,' she added, running her depressed finger over the ancient wood. 'How long has that been here, eh? They need to get their act together these people.'

'I enjoyed the table.'

'Don't want to rain on your parade but this forest furniture is a health and safety bombshell.'

Pilgrim had now lost all sense of wonder and much of her will to live.

'I suppose I could walk with you,' said Dismal.

'No,' said Pilgrim, feeling that was a bad idea.

'After all, how can things get any worse?'

'They can get worse, Dismal, by you walking with me. I find your negative presence quite disabling.'

'I'm just telling it as it is. If that's a problem – '

'No, Dismal, you're not telling it as it is, you're telling it as you perceive it to be; there's a difference. You must be very angry to be so depressed. And who made you so angry is the obvious question to be answered. But it's your issue, not mine.'

'I'm not angry.'

'And this isn't a snow-covered mountain. Goodbye, Dismal.'

And with that, Pilgrim walked on and began slowly to recover her soul. For a while she followed a sparkling mountain stream through a dense forest with pine-carpet overlay. Here she enjoyed the last light of the day in golden shafts through the branches and banks covered with purple and white dwarf snowbells.

'*It is hard to believe that such beauty could be created and seen only by me!*' she wrote.

But after the wonder and warmth of the day, the clear night sky brought a chill to the air. And Pilgrim was hungry. Where was food to be found in a place such as this? And where would she sleep? She'd been told to trust the path but it hadn't always proved kind and, as she dwelt on that thought, other fears assembled themselves. Should she have taken up Dismal's offer? Was she stupid to be walking this darkening path alone with only the howling wolves for company? The wolves could no longer be ignored, their night shrieks terrifying and close. And further on, when she saw two merciless eyes glinting in the moonlit dark, she froze with fear. What chance did she have here? And when the eyes appeared to move nearer, she simply turned and ran, dodging the trees, slipping and sliding in icy undergrowth, launching herself forward, again and again, keeping going, keeping moving through the cold.

Breathless, Pilgrim reached the edge of a scree where the land fell away. She stopped and dared look round. Was she being followed? Had she managed to shake off her pursuer? She'd heard nothing behind as she stormed through the woods, but the news was not good: two eyes had now become eight and from one of their mouths emerged another heart-stopping howl. In terror, Pilgrim threw herself down the loose-stoned scree, rolling and falling; it was halfway down that the changing vista revealed a log cabin ahead with a light burning inside. But could she get there in time?

There were now four baying wolves behind her, panting in the chase with Pilgrim plunging forwards and aware now of disturbance. Shouts were breaking out in the darkness and stones flying over her head.

'Keep running!' cried a voice holding a lantern, and Pilgrim did as bid. She ran towards the light, aware of both snarl and whimper in the snow behind.

She arrived at speed into the arms of a large man launching everything he could at the sharp-fanged pursuers, now turning back towards the dark undergrowth.

'Fear nothing,' he said, guiding her exhausted frame towards the bright red front door. 'They won't be back tonight.'

'Thank you,' said Pilgrim. 'I thought I was done for then.'

'Not an uncommon thought. We often think our story is over – '

' – until we realise it isn't?'

'Precisely. My name's Mr Home Fires by the way and welcome to the House of Joy.'

He opened the door and Pilgrim, on stepping into the light and warmth, collapsed instantly.

The fourteenth stage

Pilgrim sat settled on the sofa. She held in her hands a large mug of hot chocolate and was warming nicely. Mr Home Fires, all apron, red face and beard, had been in and out of the kitchen with both speed and efficiency and was now depositing fresh logs, still glistening with snow, in the hearth.

'The fire's hungry tonight!' he said, as the wind raged outside. 'But these must dry a little first.'

'Those wolves,' said Pilgrim. 'Would they have killed me?'

'The Wolves of Fear?'

'Is that what they were?'

'Yes, they smell it in us and then they multiply.'

'Two eyes quickly became eight.'

'Typical. After which they hunt as a pack until there's no sanity left in us, just mad terror. So yes, the Wolves of Fear cripple and kill in their way.'

Pilgrim and Home Fires were not alone in the House of Joy. This was a house party of four, the two other guests being Happy, in the large chair by the fire, and Veronica, sitting on the clown's shoulder. Pilgrim found particular delight in seeing Happy again and her recent fears melted away as she listened to him tell his surprising story:

'The first time round nobody ever told me I could be a child for ever,' he said. Veronica now moved down to his lap, which offered her a more comfortable place to stretch out.

'I was led to believe that play and discovery had to stop,' he continued. 'The message that came across loud and clear was this: "Grow up! Be responsible! Be unhappy just like the rest of us!"'

Pilgrim was intrigued to hear him talking in this way.

'The first time round I didn't question the voice of the grown-ups, never; not even when their inconsistencies left my insides churning and my mind confused. I didn't question them but I soon learned not to trust them – or myself. And without trust, fear flooded my being and took control.'

'The Wolves of Fear?'

'If you like, yes, and then there followed the forgetting and I became one of the walking dead.'

'The walking dead? How do you mean?'

'I forgot who I was. Life became automatic and I took my place in hell with all the other zombies, marching in line, following my own mad programming. Existing, surviving but not living.'

'But you were a clown at this time?'

'Oh yes, the crowd was loving the show but the joy of being was lost to me. I had entered the world of small gods, each vying for attention and place. A world which said: lie the best, earn the most, feel the least.'

'So what happened?'

'Well, it might sound odd but I began to hear another voice.'

'Weird!' said Pilgrim.

'Quiet at first; in fact so quiet I had to stop to hear it. But there it was.'

'And what did the voice say?'

'Wake up, Look, Notice, Listen.'

'And did you?'

'That voice changed many things over time. It was like I became Happy walking beside Happy.'

'You mean you were watching yourself?'

'That's right, I was watching my own actions. And the more I watched, the more I realised the suffering I caused myself. And of course I passed this suffering on to others.'

'Remind me to tell you about Dismal.'

'But then came the defining "Aha!" moment!' said Happy in an almost trance-like state.

The ever-busy Home Fires was stilled, listening intently; Veronica lazing but alert.

'What happened?'

'It was the voice again,' said Happy.

'Saying what?'

'Life does not need to be like this, life was never intended to be this difficult, stop fighting and allow life to lead the way, all is well.'

'The voice had broken through the mental nonsense!' said Home Fires.

'It had, yes. I started to let go of my opinions, my learned definitions of good and bad. Suddenly I had space for fresh perceptions. Whatever happens, I thought, I have the choice to live it well.'

'Hear, hear!' said Home Fires.

'I discovered I could learn from all experiences. I gained wisdom from being open to life and transforming the hurt I felt. And so it was I left the first time round and arrived at the second time round!'

'You describe the first and second half of life?'

'That's right – the second half of life where life is simpler and where I know nothing.'

'Nothing?'

'Well, nothing apart from the truth that I'm involved in the mystery that includes all others and that somehow this is OK, exciting even. I'm open to discovery and, in a way, every day is playtime.'

'That's a good approach,' said Home Fires, putting another log on the fire. 'I could do with a little more of that spirit in my day.'

'But!' said Happy with warning in his voice. 'This time round I have no desire to play the old games.'

'What sort of old games?' asked Pilgrim.

'Oh, you know, "tit-for-tat", "beat your neighbour" or "woe is me". Instead of reaching outside myself for security, I now reach inside. I'm ready to love and to allow myself to be loved.'

There was silence in the House of Joy apart from crackling

flames and the weight of the snow pressing on the creaking roof.

'So what now?' asked Veronica.

'A different path, the path of kindness and gentleness. I recognise this is the way. I have no rule book, I've had enough of those, but wherever I go and whoever I'm with, I know I stand on holy ground. Heaven is exactly where we're standing. Wake up, Look, Notice, Listen.'

The group parted after that, each needing time to themselves. Home Fires played the piano, Happy read a book about Oliver Cromwell, a lifelong interest, Veronica slept on his lap, and more deeply with each turn of the page, while Pilgrim lay thoughtful on the sofa and watched the steady fall of snow through the heart-shaped windows.

It was only later that night a further conversation unfolded, started by Pilgrim who'd been thinking about the path she was trying to trust.

'Where does the path lead?' asked Pilgrim. 'Anyone know? And don't just say "heaven"!'

She remembered Home Fires pausing at the piano keys and coming over to join them again.

'The path leads to that which you most deeply want,' he said.

'Oh, I see,' said Pilgrim, a little shaken.

She sat looking into the hearth. What was it she was looking for?

'So what do you most want?' asked Home Fires.

'I want so many things.'

'Of course you do. But is there one thing above all else?'

'Well – '

'Yes?'

Home Fires had produced hot soup and fresh rolls for them all except Veronica, who, now fully awake, had ordered cheese on toast with a poached egg on top.

'I want love,' said Pilgrim.

'Wonderful!' said Mr Home Fires, wiping some melted butter from his shirt. 'You want love, Pilgrim? Then you must become love, for love finds love, love grasps love.'

'That's all very well,' said Pilgrim. 'But how do you become love?'

Everyone was eating, mouths full of food, which left a short pause in the conversation, but the world did not end. In some company, silence brings fear, the sense the sky will fall in unless someone speaks; but not here.

'You trust the path and greet each kindness along the way,' said Veronica, looking up from her cheddar-fest, whiskers clogged with yolk.

'Thank you!' said Happy, slapping her a little too hard and sending her face into the egg.

Home Fires roared with laughter but Pilgrim was not in the mood. Something less cheerful was rising inside her.

'Why are you thanking Veronica?' she asked with a note of impatience.

'Why?' said Happy. 'Because she makes more sense of my journey than anyone has ever done!'

Pilgrim sat sullen for awhile, ashamed of the jealousy poisoning her veins. She wanted to be the one to help Happy make sense of his journey and was pained by every ounce of credit given to Veronica.

'Is there something on your mind?' asked Home Fires.

'No,' said Pilgrim, sipping her unhappy soup.

There was much on her mind. But how could she speak of the sickly stain running through her soul? And from where inside her did such feelings arise?

'Is that "No" as in "Yes"?' asked Home Fires.

It was at this moment that Pilgrim became aware of the child. The ghostly girl was standing at the edge of the circle, trying to warm herself by the fire. Something revolted in Pilgrim.

'Oh, for God's sake, why can't you leave me alone!' she shouted, slamming her cup of soup on the table, spilling it everywhere. 'Can't I go anywhere without you?'

The child jumped back. She stood nervous and watchful in the shadows like a frightened fox.

'I've got my own life to lead,' said Pilgrim to herself. 'I can't look after her as well. It's not fair!'

Her outburst surprised her friends. They kept a gentle silence.

'You're OK, Pilgrim' said Veronica after a while. 'There's nothing to fear here.'

'How would you know?' said Pilgrim.

'You're always safe with Mr Home Fires.'

The fire danced in shadows on the ceiling.

'Let me make some coffee,' said Happy.

He walked across to the stove.

'I know I'm safe here,' said Pilgrim, 'and you've all been very kind. It's just that – oh, what's the point? I'll never get to heaven. One step forward, two steps back. Dismal was right, that's how it is with me.'

'I know the feeling,' said Happy, sorting out a tray of cups. 'I was so down a while back I nearly returned to Headspin and the Mental Circus.'

Pilgrim was shocked.

'You never!' said Pilgrim.

'I did. I nearly went back there.'

'What? Even though he'd had you beaten up?'

'It sounds mad.'

'It is mad, completely mad!'

'But also familiar,' said Happy.

'And familiar sometimes seems like a friend,' added Veronica, who'd now managed to wash most of the egg off her face.

'And he was your first love, of course,' said Home Fires, stoking the fire again.

Happy nodded.

'And your first love is always the hardest love to leave.'

'I suppose so,' said Pilgrim. 'But there's no way I'd do that. I'd never go back.'

And then the bombshell.

'Before morning comes, Pilgrim, you'll do just that,' said Veronica.

A shocked silence filled the room.

'I'll do what?'

'Before the dawn breaks in the eastern sky, you'll deny the journey three times and start your return.'

'Absolutely no way,' said Pilgrim. 'Not in a thousand years. I've come much too far!'

And Pilgrim was so sure, she repeated it several times.

'I won't turn back,' she said. 'Not in a thousand years.'

Conversation turned to other things. In time, Home Fires brought out his flute and whistle and played some sea shanties while Happy juggled some apples and spun dinner plates on his fingers. Even Veronica got in on the act. In the flickering fire light, she performed a tap dance on the table. She called it a tap dance, though rats' feet scratch more than tap. Home Fires then produced brandy for everyone, after which bed beckoned as the winds quietened outside.

'Perhaps a late-night walk would be a good idea,' said Pilgrim. 'Some fresh air might clear my head.'

'Don't be out too long,' said Home Fires. 'It's a cold one tonight.'

'I'll be careful,' she said. 'And I'm sorry I haven't been very good company. You all deserve better.'

'No, you deserve better,' said Home Fires. 'And I'm sorry that what you deserve has not yet come to find you. Good night everyone! We'll consider the washing up in the morning.'

And with that, Pilgrim left the House of Joy and slipped out into the night.

The fifteenth stage

Pilgrim was lost in the winter wood. She hadn't meant to stay out long. The snow was falling thick and wet on her face and she'd been about to return to the House of Joy when she heard the moan; a distant cry hanging briefly in the cold night air. Always curious, Pilgrim had taken a small diversion from the path and then realised she was lost. Tall evergreens towered over her, each one alike, while fresh snow covered her footprints forbidding the retracing of steps. A deathly hush prevailed, a deep forest silence and then the moan again, this time louder.

'Is that you, Pippa?' said a weak voice.

Who here could know her name? Pilgrim made her way forward, heart racing. Lying huddled on the ground was a small old man, his coat pulled tight around him.

'Yes, it's me,' said Pilgrim.

'I'm so glad I found you. Time was running out, you see.'

'Time's not running out. You'll be fine when we get you to a fire.'

'No, not for me; time's running out for you, Pippa. You've lost your way and I've come to take you home.'

Puzzled, Pilgrim helped the figure to his feet and began to walk with him through the forest.

'Do you know where we're going?' she asked.

'I'm pretty good from here, yes,' he replied.

'That's good,' she said. 'I was completely lost!'

He seemed a sweet old man, chatting about this and that, though Pilgrim was surprised at how quickly he left his moans and groans behind. And in truth, he was neither as small nor frail as he'd first appeared. He seemed to grow a foot in height within minutes.

'Where are we going?' said Pilgrim.

'Don't worry, I know the way,' he said. 'I've taken many people along this path.'

Such reassurance was good to hear, especially in a cold wood at midnight and Pilgrim enjoyed the company of this shy man. The snow began to ease, a warmer air replaced the cold and things were looking up. As Pilgrim wrote in her diary during a brief halt:

> *I'm liking my new friend. There's something familiar about him which is a relief after recent experiences. The House of Joy was great but slightly too truthful! (If I'm allowed to say that. Not sure.) Oh, time to go.*

Pilgrim and her companion were descending the mountain now, making their way along drier and wider paths, shaped by frequent use. Captivated by their conversation, Pilgrim quite forgot the House of Joy; though it was her who spoke most. She told her companion of her past and he proved a good listener, prompting when she forgot things, almost as if he already knew her story. Finally Pilgrim realised something:

'We've been talking all this time,' she said, 'and you haven't told me your name! You mysteriously knew my name before we met but I don't know yours.'

'And why would you want to know mine?' said the man in good natured self-deprecation. 'It's hardly important!'

Just then, Pilgrim got her first glimpse of the plain that awaited them at the foot of the mountain. There in the moonlight was a vast expanse of white sand and in the distance a long dark stain across the terrain.

'What's that darkness?' asked Pilgrim.

'That's a deep chasm that's impossible to cross.'

'Ah, the chasm at last,' thought Pilgrim dubiously.

'So what will we do?' she asked.

'Don't worry, we won't be going anywhere near it,' said her friend. 'I'm taking you home, remember.'

'Is that the same as my journey to heaven?'

'Well, if heaven isn't home, what is it?' her guide said with cheery steel.

'Fair point,' said Pilgrim.

She was happy to hand over responsibility; glad to rely on someone else for directions. And how well her companion appeared to understand her, something she couldn't say for all her friends.

'And does the plain have a name?' asked Pilgrim.

'Er, yes, the plain does have a name.'

For the first time, there was a hint of uncertainty in her companion's voice.

'And will you tell me what it is?'

'Names seem important to you, Pippa; too important, in my humble opinion!'

Her companion sounded stern but he did have a point. She had been rather pushy about names, which could be construed as impolite; childish even.

'I suppose names don't really matter that much,' she said. 'A rose by any other name would smell as sweet, eh?'

'That's better,' said her guide as the path swung round and down to leave them at ground level again. They stood facing the pre-dawn darkness of the eastern sky.

'So now you have a decision to make,' said her guide.

'A decision?'

Pilgrim hoped she'd said goodbye to those.

'So far, there's only been one path down the mountain. But now we've reached the plain, two paths offer themselves.'

'I see.'

'And I'm just enquiring as to whether you still wish to come with me.'

'Well, of course I want to come with you.'

'So you still wish to go back?'

'Go back – how do you mean?'

'I mean go back to how things were, Pippa. Go back home. "Back" and "home" – they're the same words, really. You want to turn back?'

'Oh yes,' said Pilgrim who didn't want to lose him now.

'Are you sure?'

'Definitely!'

'You'll be leaving your journey to heaven.'

'I don't think it ever existed anyway!'

As she spoke the words, the first light appeared in the eastern sky, an orange streak of glory. And Pilgrim remembered Veronica's words: 'Before the dawn breaks in the eastern sky, you'll deny the journey three times and start your return.'

'*Dear Diary*,' wrote Pilgrim hurriedly, '*so Veronica called things right. Big deal and so what?! This is my life, isn't it?*'

She was returning her diary to her pocket when once again she saw the eagle high in the sky. It hovered awhile, surveying all, and then swooped down towards them, as if to take a closer look. Her companion, who was now definitely bigger than when they first met, perhaps by three or four feet, took great offence and started throwing stones at the eagle. Pilgrim was surprised: such a mild-mannered man yet behaving like the circus louts who did the same thing. But then the bird could be irritating; no, terrifying. Only Grace had saved her from those talons in the Rock of Hidden Self. 'Be gone with you!' shouted her companion, launching rock after rock at the circling eagle and hitting the target with at least one throw.

'You must travel on, Pilgrim,' said Veronica.

'It's Pippa,' said Pilgrim.

'There's no time. You're in danger here.'

Why did this rat irritate her so?

'It's traditional to start with a greeting, Veronica, or are manners a thing of the past?' she inquired primly.

Pilgrim was sitting in the shadow of a rock, eating some dry sandwiches from her large companion's pocket. Here the paths forked, one towards the chasm and one away.

'Fortunately, we'll be taking the latter,' thought Pilgrim.

The food was poor, she knew that; she'd much rather something from Home Fires' table. But looking on the bright side, it was good to be going home and giving up on heaven. And while it was true that she sat in the shadow of the rock, larger by far was the shadow of her guide who had now grown twice as high and as wide as a bus.

'You're behaving like a turkey, Pilgrim,' said Veronica. 'All strut and fret, all offended ego.'

'Speak to the hand,' said Pilgrim, holding out her palm to the rat. 'Cos Pippa ain't listening!'

Her poor American accent sounded hollow but hopefully the rat got the message.

'You have a new friend, I see,' said Veronica.

Pilgrim looked up at the enormous figure blocking the sun from view.

'A good friend, yes,' she said. 'He understands me. Pretty perfect as it happens.'

'I don't suppose he told you his name?'

'Are names really that important? I'm beyond names now. Names are so childish. I've grown up.'

'We ought to be moving,' said her nameless companion, an increasingly restless presence and a deepening voice.

'You've lost direction,' said Veronica, 'but there's still time. Just get to the chasm.'

'Lost direction, Ratty? Or simply found a guide other than you? You wouldn't be feeling a little jealous by any chance?'

'I'm feeling only your foolishness. Old Ways, of course, has been fooling you for years.'

'Old Ways?'

'That's the name of your new bezzy mate, leading you back to the unhappiness that made you start this journey in the first place.'

Old Ways let out a roar, but already he was fading, changing, like ice to water to steam until there was nothing there. Pilgrim watched aghast.

'Just make for the chasm, Pilgrim. Hate me if you must but make for the chasm.'

'Oh, I don't hate you, Veronica, I just find you rather pathetic.'

'I disturb you, Pilgrim, as one not fond of the truth.'

'Rubbish,' said Pilgrim putting her hands over her ears and shouting 'Boloney, boloney, boloney!' And then adding: 'I can't hear you by the way!'

But Pilgrim's hands came down quickly when she saw the child, standing by her side, crying.

'Shut up, you stupid child!' she said. 'I'm not interested! Go ghost somewhere else with your shadowy presence! I've had it with all your attention-seeking.'

But there was change in the small figure. The child was not ghostly now but finding form. The ghost child could now touch.

'Take the child with you,' said Veronica. 'You can travel together. You've been avoiding her for too long and you do need to talk.'

But Pilgrim pushed the girl away and watched her stumble.

'I'm taking her nowhere. I've been through enough. You don't know what I saw in the Rock of Hidden Self!'

'Oh I do, Pilgrim, you saw what Happy saw. You saw the Truth Mirror and yourself as you truly are. It's a shock, so meditate but don't murder.'

'Murder? Who said anything about murder?' asked Pilgrim in some shock.

'Wait!' said Veronica, 'the time for talk is over. The forces of darkness are upon us.'

There was something in the voice that gripped Pilgrim.

'Stay very still,' said Veronica. 'Don't move a muscle.'

'Why not?'

'We have company.'

It was then that Pilgrim became aware of the danger. There were four shiny stones in the sand about six feet from her. Only they weren't stones, for there was malice in their glistening. They were eyes, watching, staring.

'What are those?'

'Two sand vipers. Old Ways keeps a nest of them. You never see them of course. They swim beneath the sand, able to cross whole deserts like that. They ripple the surface but nothing more. And you don't see them strike either.'

'So what do we do?' asked Pilgrim, frightened now.

'I'll distract them,' said Veronica. 'And when I do, pick up the girl and run as fast as you can. She is not your pain, believe me.'

A question came into Pilgrim's mind. Dare she ask it?

'Veronica, Old Ways never told me the name of this plain.'

'You wish to know?'

'I do, yes.'

'This is the Plain of – '

Then everything happened at once. It was all a blur and over in a few seconds, though nothing was the same thereafter.

How to describe these dire and desperate events? There's Veronica darting, the flash of gold and feathers as the eagle swoops and the twin-timed strike of the vipers. Pilgrim calls to the girl as Veronica twists in the air in pain. The eagle targets the rat but misses and catches one of the snakes instead. The talons clutch at the neck but fail to hold the writhing length which attacks the child. The bird is now in Pilgrim's face and she lashes out, landing a clean and bone-breaking strike on the bird's neck. The damaged bird now grabs Veronica in its claws and lifts her up and away, carrying her helpless skywards.

Pilgrim is running with the child, dragging her by her hair, but the girl is screaming, her hobbling ankle swollen with snake venom.

'I don't like you!' shouts the child.

'And I don't like you!'

'I want you to let go of me!'

'Then I will let go of you, happily!' shouts Pilgrim. 'Go alone and see how far you get, you ungrateful little brat!'

Their hands lose touch and soon the child is a distant figure, staggering alone to nowhere and beyond.

Pilgrim runs on until she reaches the chasm and then collapses. Where to now? The chasm is a deep crack in the land and too great a divide to leap. Pilgrim has reached the chasm you cannot cross; the chasm that marks the end of her journey and the end of herself.

And now the bird is spiralling down towards her, landing awkwardly. Veronica's body is discarded on the ground. Like a cat with a mouse, the bird will no doubt return to her later. But for Pilgrim, this is the end game in every way and, with the bird struggling, Pilgrim approaches. Things are different now, the balance of power altered. Veronica is moving feebly; perhaps she can yet be saved. But Pilgrim must first destroy the bird; it's time for this quarrel to drink more blood.

And then Veronica's calling out. It's a weak cry but carries on the dry air and begs Pilgrim against violence.

'Leave him, Pilgrim – he's a friend, he's – '

But Pilgrim takes no notice. Veronica doesn't know what she's saying. She's halfway delirious and unaware of the whole story, an innocent in matters of revenge.

'This bird is no friend,' thinks Pilgrim. 'Some things you just know.'

And now Pilgrim is inching closer to her stricken prey. She watches the eagle stumble and lurch as if slightly drunk. Seizing her moment, Pilgrim grabs the bird's leg and with all her strength swings the creature against the rock, smashing hard again and again, yanking and smashing, yanking and smashing until resistance ebbs and dies and the bloodied feathers fight no more.

It is finished.

Exhausted, and with eagle blood on her hands, Pilgrim wandered over to where Veronica lay. She was growing spastic with pain, hunching and twisting, speech strange and mouth distorted by the swelling of the viper's bite.

'You've killed my dearest friend,' she said.

'Don't get sentimental about the bird,' replied Pilgrim, still sweating from the assault. 'She's been after you and me from the beginning. If I hadn't hurt her back there, you'd be high in the skies now with her claws in your side.'

'How little you know!'

'Oh really?' said Pilgrim with heavy sarcasm.

'It was "the bird", as you call him, who saw you in trouble on the cliff with the tigers and sent me to help.'

'What?'

'And it was "the bird" – whose real name is Jesse, by the way – who feared you'd get sidetracked by Happy in the mountain and sent the nurse to your side.'

'Oh, I don't think so!'

'And finally, it was Jesse who tried to save me back there, attacking the snake and taking its poison.'

Pilgrim felt the heat of shame coursing through her veins.

'Are you sure?'

'It doesn't matter now,' said Veronica. 'What's done is done and know this, nothing is always so.'

The rat choked a little and her whiskers twitched. With her middle finger, Pilgrim stroked Veronica's head and dumbo ears. Through the thin fur she felt her beating heart and, as she felt Veronica's, Pilgrim felt her own.

'Many hearts but one heart beat, eh?' she said.

Was that a smile on Veronica's face?

'Old Ways never told me the name of this plain,' whispered Pilgrim.

'He wouldn't, would he?' choked Veronica. 'It's called the Plain of False Assumption and it's been the death of many.'

'Is it the death of me?'

'In a way, Pilgrim, in a way.'

She felt her stomach churn.

'It's the death of you but not the end of you,' said Veronica. 'There's a difference.'

'I can't imagine what,' said Pilgrim.

'You will not need to imagine, you will know. But before we say goodbye – '

'Yes?'

Veronica again went into spasm.

'Before we … goodbye, Pilgrim.'

'Veronica!'

But the rat was quite still.

Pilgrim sat in shock for a while, holding Veronica in her lap. Sometimes life stops for the living as well as the dead. Pilgrim noticed a small flower growing by her side and some ants busy with a crust that had fallen from her pocket. And then slowly, and after a while, she placed the lifeless body on the ground. She had no experience of desert burial, it didn't happen every day. She knew only that all would be done with due honour and respect. She took out her handkerchief and wrapped it carefully round the limp body, a burial shroud. She then dug a hole with her hands, kissed Veronica's corpse and placed it in the hole. She gazed on it for a while before covering her over. She chose a small rock as the headstone as hot tears broke from her eyes and down her face.

'I know it's too late, Veronica, a thousand years too late but thank you.'

What now?

Afternoon was turning to dusk as Pilgrim returned to the dead bird, crucified by false assumption. But then the shock! For as she returned to the rock where the eagle had died, there was no eagle. In its place was a human form, beaten like the bird, bloodied and broken and with the same pendant round his neck.

Lying before Pilgrim was a dead man, and one she recognised. '*Dear Diary*', she wrote in a shaky hand, '*I have killed* Will *Good.*'

The sixteenth stage

Pilgrim wished to run away but instead moved closer. Drawn by the chain and tag round Will's neck, Pilgrim edged cautiously towards the body. Kneeling down, she took the small gold pendant in her hand and gazed on the inscription:

'Will Good was beloved of the earth?' thought Pilgrim. 'Then God help the rest of us.'

And on turning away, she found a weeping willow nearby and sat down.

'Forgive me, please,' she whispered to the sad sky. 'I did not now what I was doing. Look down on me with kindness, please.'

But the sky did not hear her and Pilgrim knew the journey to heaven, begun in such hope, meant nothing now. She began to write.

> *What did Veronica mean when she said it was the death of me but not the end of me? Surely death and the end are one? But what does it matter anyway? I'm now Pilgrim the famous murderer and quite beyond the reach of goodness.*

Here beneath the willow was her dark night of the soul; the end of every hope and dream, the collapse of every wish and plan. Pilgrim felt like a cracked pot through which all life had leaked away. There was nothing in this darkness but what was; and what was, was too terrible to contemplate. She sat and cried like she'd never cried before. Tears flowed like a river down her body, forming rivulets in the dust by her side. She barely noticed that in the watered soil, poppies grew pink and red, purple and white.

When the tears ceased, there was calm. And she found herself writing further words in her diary, strange words.

> *I sit here beneath the weeping willow as dusk gives way to night. I'm weary, confused, cold, hungry and a long way from home. But despite all that, it's as though I must be here in this darkness. Why? I don't know and it makes no sense. It simply feels like I must be here, that this is the truest place I've ever been, a dazzling darkness. It swallows whole the cosy inventions of my imagination but offers something fresh in return. It makes no sense.*

Pilgrim's crazed jottings beneath the weeping willow were interrupted.

'Hello', said a smart young woman.

'Hello', said Pilgrim, barely stirring.

'You look a little down.'

'Really?' said Pilgrim caustically. 'I can't imagine why.'

'I've done a counselling course,' said the woman.

'Is that so?'

'I notice these things. Body language reveals so much.'

Pilgrim took a few deep breaths before continuing.

'Well, that's all very observant of you, I'm sure, but I'm not "a little down" as you say.'

'You're not? Then mildly unhappy perhaps or slightly off-colour?'

'Neither.'

'Then what are you?'

'I'm in hell,' said Pilgrim, deciding it was best to be honest.

The young woman looked puzzled.

'How so?'

'You mean what have I done to get there?'

'Yes, I'm feeling around for the issue here, as we counsellors do.'

'Well, the issue is mainly that I killed Will Good.'

'Who was he?'

'Good question.'

'I like to think so.'

'Will Good was both the start of my journey to heaven and the one who looked after me along the way.'

'OK.'

'And if that doesn't sound like a good reason to kill him, well, it isn't! It's just the dreadful truth.'

'Now steady on there, traveller,' said the woman with a smile, 'and less of the dreadful. I've got good news for you.'

Pilgrim stared blankly ahead.

'It'll need to be very good,' she said, running her fingers through the poppies.

'Well try this: there's no such place as heaven! And no such place as hell!'

'Really?'

'They simply don't exist. So don't get wound up about it all.'

Pilgrim was interested in her words but had a question.

'Who are you?' she asked, believing a word cannot be judged a true word until you know who speaks it and how they use it.

'My name's Millicent.'

'Unusual.'

'Millicent Atheist.'

'I'm Pilgrim. Pippa Pilgrim.'

'And I left that faith nonsense behind a long time ago. Life's really much better without it.'

'Is that so?'

'Undoubtedly,' said Millicent. 'I mean, the whole belief thing's a shambles from beginning to end. So many religions! So many gods! I mean, they can't all be right, can they?'

'Well – '

'And then there's the appalling things believers do in the name of their so-called gods, which, as psychologists have shown, are in fact merely egoic projections of needy people in search of a father figure and meaning in a completely meaningless universe.'

'I always thought – '

'And, I mean, look at the trouble religion has caused in the world!' continued Millicent, pressing Pilgrim up against the tree. 'Endless war, endless torture and – speaking woman to woman – endless repression of women.'

Pilgrim knew how they felt.

'And here's the killer question,' said Millicent, 'If there is a god of love, and it's an "if" without any scientific backing, how could such a god allow suffering? See my point? Exactly!'

Millicent said 'exactly' as though Pilgrim had replied with something like 'How indeed? The idea's quite ridiculous.' But she hadn't said that or indeed anything else, being too shell-shocked by the tirade which now continued.

'And furthermore, if there is a god, which there isn't, but if there was, he – '

'Or she,' said Pilgrim. 'We probably shouldn't be sexist here, even if she doesn't exist.'

'He or she,' continued Millicent, 'if they existed, would have to be a complete and utter sadist! Fact! Or just very, very weak. So let's be honest, Pilgrim, there's simply no good reason to believe. I'm a free thinker who demands the empirical evidence of science. Are you a free thinker who demands the empirical evidence of science?'

Pilgrim wasn't sure on either count, but there was no time for an answer anyway.

'And don't you find religions so pushy?' said Millicent, pinning her further back against the willow with her jabbing finger.

'They can be a little – '

'I find them unbearably pushy, as I'm sure you do.'

'Er – '

'Well do you find them pushy or don't you?'

'I – '

'Yes or no? YES OR NO? I mean it's not a complicated question!'

Millicent's face was now six inches from Pilgrim's.

'I'm not an expert in these things,' said Pilgrim, extracting herself from imprisonment and finding a nearby stone on which to sit.

'No, you're not.'

'And I can't disagree with anything you've said,'

'That's true.'

'And I'm aware you say you have the scientists behind you with their white coats and improbable evidence – '

'– empirical evidence.'

'Indeed. But you know what?'

'What?'

'I'm still left wondering.'

'Wondering? How can you be wondering? I couldn't have been clearer!'

'I'm wondering why sometimes I feel joy or sadness or hope?'

'That's easy, Pilgrim,' said Millicent with a weary smile. 'Chemical reaction in the brain. Fact.'

Pilgrim took this in with a contemplative nod.

'And then there's beauty,' she said. 'I mean, look at the sky.'

They looked up at the vast desert sky above them, a luminous black blanket they could almost touch and sewn with a thousand sparkling jewels. Pilgrim particularly noted the orange hue of Jupiter tonight.

'How is it that I can appreciate such beauty?' asked Pilgrim.

'More chemicals,' said Millicent.

'Maybe. And then of course there's kindness, empathy, warmth, discernment, courage, curiosity, depth, spaciousness, sacrifice, happiness, openness, gentleness, friendship, wonder, justice, comedy, contentment and generosity.'

There was a pause as the free thinker thought as freely as she was able in the circumstances.

'Chemicals,' said Millicent.

Pilgrim smiled.

'Well, if that is true, my friend, respect is due to the one who made such variable and life-enhancing chemicals, eh? And also to the one who made the chemicals which allow you to think so freely, as you say. Not that I'm an expert.'

Pilgrim got up from the stone and brushed herself down. She couldn't be sure, but were these perhaps the first green shoots of life she was feeling inside her?

'So you'll continue your ridiculous journey to heaven?' asked Millicent.

'I think I might, Millicent,' said Pilgrim. 'And you're welcome to join me for a while. We travel alone but meet friends along the way.'

'I don't think so, if it's all the same to you. Heaven probably sucks anyway. Lots of angel wings and loud singing, isn't it?'

'We'll see. One step at a time. Goodbye Millicent.'

Pilgrim walked on. She knew she should be feeling downhearted but the meeting with Millicent had left her strangely warmed, despite the parting shot delivered beneath the stars:

'We're just chemicals, you know!'

Soon after, Pilgrim heard a strange sound. Somewhere up ahead, bells clinked weakly. What bells could be ringing in the desert? As she got closer, things became clearer. She heard the 'baa, baa' of sheep, or were they goats? And after travelling a little further, a tent came into view with a fire burning. Sitting on the ground by the hot blaze was the shepherd, a man of deep black skin. Sensing her approach he rose and with strong, graceful movement came across to meet her. Pilgrim knew with whom she spoke, though neither at first said a word.

Indeed, his first act was to bow and his second to lead her gently across to the fire where he sat her down beside the warmth. He disappeared inside the tent and returned with red wine, wild mushrooms and goat's cheese and then made desert bread in the embers of the fire. Pilgrim ate hungrily and sipped thoughtfully beneath the big sky.

'Pointy sends his regards,' she ventured. 'He said if I met you to pass them on.'

Word Shy smiled.

'I first met him by the sunflowers in the Garden of Sadness and then again by the Rock of Hidden Self. As soon as he knew I was coming here, he thought of you. You must have made an impression.'

Word Shy looked sad, though maybe he was happy. With some faces, it's hard to tell and so it was with this shepherd. Indeed, he seemed to look through happiness and sadness to something elusive beyond them both.

'But all that seems a long time ago now,' continued Pilgrim, aware once again of her situation. 'A lifetime really and I don't know what's become of him since.'

Pilgrim felt the wine warming her stomach.

'What's become of me, however, is this.'

She felt the need for honesty and Word Shy would be her confessor.

'Somewhere along the way, and I don't know why or where it happened, I got a little lost, missed a few signs. And that's putting it politely.'

Word Shy gave no clue as to his thoughts and they shared the desert silence for a while. It was a safe silence and soon Pilgrim was pouring words into it:

'Pointy did warn me that I shouldn't expect a long conversation with you. He said you believe you have only seven words to speak before you die. It doesn't seem a lot but then I suppose you just choose them carefully. Maybe we should all have a limit on the words we speak! I think I could have used some of mine more wisely.'

So many conversations came to Pilgrim's mind.

'Not that I'm looking for any words,' said Pilgrim. 'What can verbiage do for me now? I think I'm a little beyond all that.'

Word Shy disappeared into the tent and Pilgrim wondered if that was goodbye. After all, what could he say? He wouldn't want to use up any of his precious words on her. But he returned carrying a cushion and blanket which he laid over her. She was desperately tired and, with her head on the desert pillow, she felt herself drifting. But not before hearing what she never thought she'd hear.

'All's quite well,' said Word Shy. 'Trust.'

They were the best four words Pilgrim had ever heard.

Sleep.

Pilgrim was being carried through the night both by Word Shy and by silence. It was all she wanted. In times past when desperate, she'd sought the numbing noise of people's words, the distracting exchange of ideas, comment and jokes. But now she wanted only the strong silence of this desert shepherd and the stillness of the big sky above.

If she'd been asleep by the fire, she was wide awake now, lifted and carried forward. And they were crossing the chasm. They must have walked alongside it for a while but now Pilgrim was being carried over. How, she wasn't sure. She felt the big drop below and smelt the stale air wafting up from its belly, as if her old life was rotting there; beyond that she knew nothing but her safe passage over. She'd made it to the chasm you couldn't cross and was now crossing it. Again Veronica's words returned:

'It's the death of you but not the end of you.'

Then others were joining them. Pilgrim and Word Shy had reached the other side, were back on solid ground but she was now aware of people around her. She was still held by the shepherd but this group carried another body, held above their heads, the body of Will Good blessed by the light of the mourning moon. They sang as they walked, songs of sadness, remembrance and hope. And the poppies again, soft poppies, gentle poppies of witness, red and purple, pink and white. They grew wherever a tear fell and stretched as far as the eye could see.

'Though I pass through the valley of the shadow of death,' said Pilgrim, 'I shall fear no evil for your rod and your staff, they comfort me.'

She said it again and again and again.

And beyond the poppy fields, the sea. How much time had

passed she couldn't tell, and perhaps she'd slept. But now she heard the sea lapping on the shore and the crowd quietening. She smelt salty air, touched wet sand, heard the piercing screams of gulls overhead and watched as a large stone was rolled back from a cave entrance.

What cave was this? The question became answer as the body of Will Good was carried inside and laid in the darkness of this rocky womb. The carriers then left and with effort and strain, the large stone was pushed forward again. Pilgrim heard the crunch of impact, stone on stone, locking the granite grave. Sealed inside lay the body of kindness and strength, one who in life had flown so high yet swooped so low; who'd ridden the wind and taken the blows; a beach tomb for Will Good, and finally his body at rest.

The mourners' songs rose again into the night, a crescendo of agony and distress. But in time the laments faded, leaving Pilgrim alone on the beach, lying in the dunes.

'Good bye, Will, goodbye Word Shy,' she heard herself say.

And after that, she remembered nothing more.

The seventeenth stage

They looked together at the distant horizon. Pointy had woken Pilgrim from her sandy slumbers and after giving her some rum continued with his dancing.

'So do you hear the music now?' asked Pointy, returning to her side.

Pilgrim listened again but sadly shook her head.

'That's quite all right,' said Pointy.

'Will it be brass, strings or mainly choral?' she asked.

'None of those, really,' said Pointy. 'But you'll know it when you hear it.'

'So you say.'

'Indeed I do.'

'So what's out there?' asked Pilgrim, wishing to change the subject.

'That's the Beyond Land.'

They were looking out to the sea which seemed to beckon.

'Have you ever been there?' asked Pilgrim.

'Not particularly.'

'Not particularly? How can you "not particularly" have been somewhere?'

'Easy.'

'No, it's not easy. Either you have been there or you haven't.'

'Well, if that's the choice then I haven't.'

'You haven't?'

'No.'

'You haven't been to the Beyond Land?'

'I haven't been to the Beyond Land.'

'Are you quite sure?'

'This is getting dull.'

'But if you haven't been there, how can you guide me there?'

'I can't.'

'I mean, surely a guide must have travelled further than the one who follows?'

'I refer you to my last answer.'

'The guide is one further down the path, but you – '

Pilgrim stopped, finally registering Pointy's words.

'What do you mean, you can't guide me?'

'This is where we part.'

'Where we part? But I need your help on the journey.'

'No, the journey is your help. Keep walking – '

'– and the path will come and find me. Yes, I remember. But how exactly does the path find me in the sea?'

Pointy shrugged. He was losing interest, which irritated Pilgrim. Guides should be committed to those they guide but Pointy's commitment and wisdom had proved sporadic at best. And as she watched him fuss about with his braces she realised something else about Pointy: he was really, really vain.

'And another thing,' she said, 'why haven't you been there? Why haven't you been to the Beyond Land?'

'I must leave.'

'You can't leave before telling me!'

'Oh, I can.'

Pointy began to spin on his toes once again.

'Oh, please tell me!' shouted Pilgrim calling out to the disappearing figure.

Pointy struck a stationary pose for a moment.

'You haven't noticed the sea?' he called out.

'What about it?'

'I like solid ground beneath my feet.'

'You're frightened of a little water?'

'That's a lot of water.'

'And calm as a mill pond!'

This was true. With the sun setting in the West, there could be no more peaceful view than the one which lay before them both.

'You don't know much,' said Pointy. 'But you will!'

'How do you mean?'

'Goodbye, my friend,' said Pointy. 'We do what we can and I've done what I can.'

'You've been very helpful,' shouted Pilgrim, not wishing to appear ungrateful.

'No, my life has passed like a misspent half-hour, but it's done now, time for that old curtain to fall.'

'Don't say that!'

'But yours, Pilgrim? Your life has many miles to go. So rest, rise and run – for every step is a kiss!'

She watched in silence as he danced a little further along the beach, but both dance and dancer were dying. Then slowly he fell to the ground, his tired legs buckling. His pirouettes were past as he became still with the sand and one with the dust. The baggy clothes blew in the wind but the body inside was spent.

'Goodbye, Pointy,' whispered Pilgrim.

And then she sat by the cave entrance and scribbled in her notebook:

> *I've just said goodbye to Pointy. He wasn't that wise, given that he was a guide. He was also rather vain about his appearance and, to be honest, a little preoccupied with himself generally. But he met me along the path and pointed me in ways I couldn't see for myself. So thank you, Pointy. But every step a kiss? Mmmm …*

Pilgrim put her notebook away and looked towards the distant horizon. Where to now? Will Good's tomb was behind her, and in front of her a huge expanse of water. She was feeling calm if unknowing when terror like a flash-flood returned: the child was on the beach and running into the sea.

'Come back!' shouted Pilgrim. 'You'll drown!'

But the child ran on through the water, determined, splashing and disappearing from view. Pilgrim sprinted across the sand and into the water after her. It was cold as an ice bucket, shocking the breath out of her. But there was no sign of the child; not even in the small boat bobbing on the water.

'Where has she gone?' wondered Pilgrim.

Not wishing to give up, she chose the boat as a search craft and climbed in. It was good to be out of the water and, released from the mooring pole, the boat became free on the sea.

Pilgrim was no oarswoman, however, revealed by the fact that within two minutes of her maiden voyage, she'd lost both oars. They now floated some way from the boat and appeared in no hurry to return.

'This boat business is not as easy as it looks,' noted Pilgrim before becoming aware of the consequences. Looking back to land, Pilgrim was shocked at how far she'd drifted and was unsure now how to return.

Apart from the absent oars, the rowing boat was equipped only with a pile of tarpaulin, useful perhaps in a storm. Pilgrim also found a plastic bag in which she wrapped her diary but nothing else until looking beneath her seat she made a most surprising discovery.

'That's me!' she cried out to the seagulls.

And indeed it was. Here in watercolours, gazing out at her, was a picture of herself when younger, the one that hung on her wall at home. It was an idealised picture, painted by a street artist with an eye to please. If she was honest, she'd never been quite that calm, confident and sophisticated; but it had been a good self-image to take into the world.

'Until now,' thought Pilgrim.

With a few hiccups in life, she'd maintained a pretty good self-image along the way. This had meant pretence, of course, bucket loads of that, but everything had been manageable until the whole murder business; that had rather ruined things. And then another thought struck her, a realisation that made her heart skip a beat and her neck prickle. The picture resembled her now. How could it not? But the person it resembled most was not her but the child.

The child! Pilgrim was adrift in the sea searching not for any child but for her childhood self, rejected on numerous occasions since the journey began and last seen disappearing into deep water.

'How could I not have recognised her before?' she said beneath her breath.

'Easily done,' came the reply. 'Easily done.'

Pilgrim looked round. The boat was empty but the sea which lapped at the side of the craft contained a fish which seemed to have his eye on her.

'Was that you?' asked Pilgrim.

'Just an observation,' said the fish.

'And a kind one,' she said, surprised at how easily she entered into conversation with a mackerel. 'I don't handle blame well.'

'It's a big discovery, the one you've just made.'

'You could say that, yes,' said Pilgrim wiping a tear from her eye. 'I'm sorry but you've caught me at a rather emotional moment.'

Pilgrim's heart was beating at an unusual rate and she felt the opposite of calm, confident and sophisticated.

'I just didn't want you punishing yourself,' said the fish.

'Then we should have met twenty years ago.'

'No, you wouldn't have listened then. You needed to live what you've lived. But now?'

At that moment a wave smacked against the boat and as Pilgrim fell forward her arm smashed against the side. The picture was knocked from her hands and went spinning into the sea.

'My picture!' she cried.

Salt water covered and consumed the floating canvas, way beyond her reach. Pilgrim watched in horror as the confident and sophisticated face began to dissolve. Hard lines became soft lines and then no lines at all as the image disappeared and became one with the sea. It felt like death and Pilgrim was finding it hard to breathe.

'That's me,' she said.

'No,' said the fish.

'You don't understand,' said Pilgrim forcefully. 'That was always me and now it isn't! I just died!'

Tears rolled down her cheeks.

'You haven't died, Pilgrim; an image of you has died.'

'It was a good image.'

'But also a pretence, so what's lost?'

'I don't see it that way.'

The fish thoughtfully swam round to the other side of the boat. Pilgrim needed some time.

'Emotions are to be taken seriously,' continued the fish.

'Thank you.'

'But not that seriously.'

'Why not? My emotions are very serious.'

'They're serious but passing, and therefore not defining.'

'What do you mean?'

'When you see a person in the street, you do not rush up to

them and say, "I am you! We are the same person!"'

'Obviously not. That would be both embarrassing and inappropriate.'

'Indeed. Yet within yourself, you do just that. You rush up to emotions and say "I am you! We are the same!" And somehow you're not embarrassed in the least.'

'So, when I'm as distraught as now?'

'Simply remember that distraught is not you. It is like a passing stranger in the street. Greet them but don't grab them. Your soul sky is blue though distraught clouds pass through.'

'Very poetic, I'm sure.'

At that moment, there was a deep rumbling beneath them all. It seemed to start on land but reached deep beneath the sea, disturbing the water, which became choppy and surging.

'What on earth is that?' asked Pilgrim suddenly clasping the side of the swaying boat.

'That'll be the resurrection of Will Good.'

'The what?'

'The resurrection of Will Good.'

'But that's impossible!'

'How so?

'I killed him. Believe me, I know. After what I did, there was no way back, I'm quite certain of that.'

'Then that may be a certainty whose time has run out.'

'How can a certainty run out of time?'

'Simple. It just stops being true any more.'

'Just like that?'

'Well don't look so surprised. Strictly speaking, of course, it was never true, just assumed to be so, like the earth being flat.'

'You mean everyone thought it was true even though it wasn't?'

'Precisely. Our lives are a series of discarded certainties. What is true in the morning is sometimes a lie in the afternoon.'

Pilgrim could not hide her shock.

'You ought to get out more,' said the fish, shaking its scaly head. 'Think about it.'

Pilgrim was trying to think about it as the boat rocked in the awkward sea.

'How can death hold life?' said the fish, leaning forward over the side of the boat. 'Death can only hold death and there's no death in Will Good. And so the earth shakes, the tomb crumbles and tectonic plates buckle and shift. Hope lives again! We are present again, divine again, saved again!'

Pilgrim slowly picked through the words, trying to understand.

'So when we are present to life – '

'– death has lost its sting. And there is plenty of life in you, Pilgrim.'

'Who are you?' asked Pilgrim, because she had been wondering.

'I'm Mick the Mindful Mackerel.'

At this point, Pilgrim sees not one but two awful things. She sees the world's largest wave approaching at speed, towering over the seascape with a cold darkness. And she sees the child emerge from under the tarpaulin and teeter dangerously on the edge of the boat.

'You stupid girl!' shouts Pilgrim. 'What on earth are you doing here?'

Rain is now falling, whipped sideways by the wind and lashing the boat; thunder explodes like collapsing mountains and sky-splitting lightning fractures the sky. Pilgrim lunges towards the girl to pull her back but is too late. The girl is gone over the side and the giant wave almost upon them.

'I'm terrified!' screams Pilgrim.

'No, you're experiencing terror,' says Mick, bobbing in the swirling sea.

'Somehow that's not helping!'

'Allow the terror, be present to it and then act freely.'

'Freely? You must be joking! There's no freedom here, no freedom in a storm such as this!'

'What must you do?' asks Mick.

And amazingly, Pilgrim, both calm and confident, knows. The wind and rain smash against her face as the small boat twists and turns on the turbulent sea, but still she knows. And as she becomes aware of her knowing, the terror is gone and a sense of freedom runs through her body.

'I must go after her,' shouts Pilgrim as lightning again splits the skies. 'It's time to find her and perhaps myself. What do you reckon?'

Pilgrim looks for Mick but he's gone. She's talking to herself.

As the wave towers over the boat, Pilgrim dives into the cold depths.

The eighteenth stage

Pilgrim is travelling down and down through the ocean, enveloped in a tornado tube of speeding water, a hollow surrounded by drowning. She's in a spinning chute of wet, wrapped in sheets of foam, all whirl-about and spin, drilling the deep places, a liquid channel of intensity now entering the ocean crust, boring through, the land beyond and down again, through earthquake nest of tilt, strain and pressure and then further below, further and further, beyond the deep rock and ancient sediment of the upper mantle, down Pilgrim goes until – space!

Pilgrim is thrown, high and turning, flying through air, and splash! Now gasping for breath and swimming, splashing and swimming in a sea beyond the sea, in a lake beneath it all, the core of the planet and the origin of life. Pilgrim feels ancient mud between her toes and smells the gentle scent of evening flowers.

The child watches Pilgrim as she emerges from the lake. There's a fire burning on the shore and the child sits on a log next to it. It's a summer's evening, warm, clear and kind. There's a spread of food on a wooden table and a kettle boiling on the fire.

'Are those potatoes baking?' asks Pilgrim, sniffing the air.

The girl nods.

'You always liked those!' says Pilgrim. 'Or rather, I always liked those. '

There's a pause as Pilgrim reaches the flames and allows the heat across her cold, tired body. And then she speaks, there's so much to say.

'I'm sorry it's been so long.'

The child remains quiet and cautious.

'I – how can I put this? – I didn't recognise you,' says Pilgrim. 'Not until I saw the picture on the boat and made the connection. Until then, I just thought you were, well, another attention-seeking youngster.'

'I was,' says the girl.

Pilgrim, struggling for words, takes a knife from the table and prods the potatoes sitting in the orange embers. The blade sinks into the soft potato flesh.

'I think they're ready', she says, eager to be eating, and soon they are.

They sit on logs and enjoy the potatoes with grated cheese, baked beans and salad. They both choose the elderflower to drink.

'And how could you be anything else when I gave you no attention?' says Pilgrim, picking up where they left off. 'When I left you and never returned.'

'I thought you'd want to meet me.'

'I did want to meet you, Pippa.'

'You hid it well.'

'I just didn't know it. Or perhaps fear blocked my knowing and blinded my seeing. Oh, I don't know! Why don't we talk about the flowers or something more cheerful!'

'Because we need to talk about us.'

Pilgrim breathes deeply. She's drying nicely. It had been some journey to this place and the unfolding dialogue was not what she'd planned. But then what on the journey had been? The girl was right, they did need to talk.

'OK,' she says. 'What can I say? For the adult, sometimes it's harder to go back than to go forward. Does that make any sense?'

'Not really.'

'You were the fear I'd never gone to, the sadness I'd never lived, the anger I'd never acknowledged. Would you embrace that figure? Honestly?'

The girl gazes out towards the lake and Pilgrim finds calm in following her. After the disturbing splash of her arrival, the water is stilling now. And as it stills, the inner reality is revealed ever more clearly.

'I know one thing,' says the girl.

'What's that?'

'You must never again fear love.'

This was not the answer Pilgrim was expecting.

'That's an odd thing to say. Where did that come from?'

'I knew you'd gone, you see, knew you'd left me when you started pretending to be all sophisticated.'

'I wasn't pretending!' says Pilgrim. 'I really was!'

'Don't worry,' said Pippa, interrupting. 'And no offence; but a lot of adults do it. You're hardly the first.'

'No offence taken,' says Pilgrim, taking offence.

'It's like they're defending themselves,' continues the girl, 'building a wall to protect themselves from the one thing that can save them.'

'And what's that?'

'True love.'

'True love? Nice idea, Pippa, but you and I both know that wasn't always around.'

'We do, yes.'

'Love was occasional and conditional.'

'No one has perfect parents.'

'So why trust something that doesn't exist?' says Pilgrim. 'You must grow up a bit. I mean, of course I pretended things. It's how you survive out there, and if you were older you'd know that. And hey! If it makes you a half-person, then that's the price you pay. Life is the School of Hard Knocks.'

Pilgrim felt she had made her point. There was a naivety in the child which was understandable but in need of correction.

'But I can still remember true love,' says the girl, 'so I don't need to pretend.'

Pilgrim was caught off balance.

'And what love is that?'

'The love I knew before I was born.'

'Before you were born?'

'You've forgotten it, I know, but I'm younger than you, closer to the sense of it than you. I haven't had to pretend anything so still know it inside, the time when God and I were one. That's all I wanted to tell you.'

They finished the meal in silence. It was a silence to die for and, in a way, they both had. They enjoyed Greek yoghurt and fruit for dessert and Pilgrim had never felt so happy in her life. After the meal, they walked with wonder in the Woods of Love and then, exhausted, lay down to rest by the smouldering remains of the fire. They'd both had a busy day with more sea air, storm and water than they were used to.

'Do you think we'll ever be parted again?' says little Pippa, gazing up at the darkening sky.

'I hope not,' replies Pilgrim embracing the child against the chill of the night.

In that embrace, they both slept a deep sleep. And had you been watching, what would you have seen? An osmosis most strange as two became one, adult and child, their hearts and bodies melding. Two figures had returned from the wood to rest. But only one heard the dawn chorus and breakfasted in the sparkling dew.

The ninteenth stage

The events of the following morning were not as expected, for the path, which surely now should become clearer, became less so.

Pilgrim had woken with a feeling of peace and contentment. For a while, she'd simply lain still, listening to the bird song and contemplating a spider hanging a few inches from her nose. She'd then fried eggs, made toast and boiled the kettle for tea on the reawakened embers of the fire.

And it was while sitting quietly after breakfast that Pilgrim heard the music of which Pointy spoke. She hadn't heard it by the sunflowers or on the beach but she heard it now, the silent music of deep wisdom, a harmonious symphony of quiet knowledge, a sounding solitude and the melody of spiritual harmony with all that is.

'So that's what you danced to, Pointy!' she thought.

And she was sitting on the same log stump, pondering life, the universe and the wonder of wood smoke when Billie the butterfly appeared from behind a purple rhododendron.

'Long time no see, Billie!' said Pilgrim cheerfully, as the butterfly made flapping and uncertain progress towards a nearby copse.

And so it was that Pilgrim arose and continued her journey to heaven. Billie led the way with her blue and orange darting, colours clearly caught in the shafts of golden light cascading through the trees. This morning's adventure was a good one and undertaken with startling energy, as if two were now harnessed to Pilgrim's purpose, and perhaps they were.

But as time went by, as has been mentioned, the fragile guidance became harder to discern and the way unclear. A creeping mist settled on Pilgrim's way, swallowing both the sun above and the path ahead. Pilgrim could now barely see her feet.

'*Who knows where it came from but a fog has suddenly fallen,*' wrote Pilgrim in the murky haze. '*And I'm concerned. I've lost the path before on this journey and do not want to do so again.*'

'Where's the path?' said Pilgrim to herself.

She breathed deeply to bring calm. There was a way forward, she knew that.

'Now where's the path?' she repeated.

'There is no path,' came the answer.

Pilgrim stood still. This was a voice she knew but couldn't see; or at least thought she knew.

'Is that you, Grace?'

'It is me, sweet one.'

Pilgrim reached out but found only mist between her fingers.

'Do not touch me, Pilgrim, you will not succeed. For like the air that you breathe, I am within and without.'

Pilgrim sat herself on a low branch and considered this new state of Grace. Anger rose up inside her and Pilgrim watched it pass through; after the anger came sadness and after the sadness, calm.

'So where am I?' she asked. 'I always seem to be somewhere on this journey!'

'You walk in the Cloud of Unknowing, my friend.'

'The Cloud of Unknowing?'

'That's right. And in this cloud, there is no path to follow.'

'Then how am I to continue my journey?' she asked. 'I feel I've come a little too far to turn back now!'

Grace chuckled with Pilgrim.

'In the Cloud of Unknowing, the path withdraws and you walk by the power and insight of your heart. The way is inside you rather than outside. From here on, Pilgrim, you and the power of your heart are the way.'

Pilgrim, both fearful and amazed, gently kicked at the dark earth of a molehill in the grass beside her.

'How things have changed,' she said.

'More than you know,' said Grace.

'How do you mean?'

She was getting used to conversation with someone she could neither see nor touch.

'You see that molehill?' said Grace.

Pilgrim looked down at her feet.

'Yes.'

'Do you fear it, Pilgrim?'

'Fear the molehill? Why would I ever fear that?'

It was a ridiculous idea and seemed the oddest of questions.

'That's the Rock of Hidden Self,' said Grace.

'No way!' protested Pilgrim.

'It is so.'

'No, no, no. The Rock of Hidden Self was utterly different, large and terrifying. I was there in its shadow!'

'It was large and terrifying to you then, Pilgrim. But it was your inner state that determined its size. Now, of course, having bravely travelled the journey you have, it appears to you as a small molehill and quite harmless. As you say, things have changed.'

Pilgrim had one more question.

'And how long until I reach the gates of heaven? Or as I used to say in the car, "Are we nearly there yet?"'

'I know nothing of time, my friend.'

'But distance?'

'Distance, yes. You are close, good and faithful Pilgrim, just a breath away.'

'Just a breath away?'

And so it was that Pilgrim walked on. She took mindful steps through the thick Cloud of Unknowing and saw with more clarity than she'd ever seen in her life. She became her own way, as Grace said it would be, walking in the power and insight of her heart. And in this manner Pilgrim journeyed on, though whether it was for five minutes, five days or five years she couldn't be sure.

The mist came and went as she walked but thick or clear, Pilgrim's journey was not greatly affected. Knowing and unknowing proved surprisingly similar and she travelled on, day and night, until she came upon a door in a wall.

She stopped and gazed on it.

'*What door is this? When unsure, I ponder,*' she wrote in her diary.

It was a solid entrance, both ancient and new yet also bent and bursting; for like an eager dog held back, there was brilliance and brightness behind this homely gate, straining at the leash, forcing itself through the cracks.

'*So close to heaven, surely?*' wrote Pilgrim.

But before she'd returned the diary to her pocket, the air chilled.

'You've been avoiding me,' said a voice.

'Is that you, Grace?' said Pilgrim.

But she knew only too well that it wasn't.

'Who are you?' she asked.

'I think you know, Pippa.'

'It's Pilgrim. My name's Pilgrim.'

'A fancy new name?'

'It's who I am.'

'How quaint. How spiritual! And I do love all things spiritual, the pleasing umbrella for so much egotistical nonsense.'

Pilgrim felt deep unease.

'So you must forgive me,' continued the voice. 'I mock your name only because I've never taken labels very seriously. Not when they're stuck on with such scant regard for the inner reality.'

Reeling from this accusation, Pilgrim tried to calm herself.

'My name is Pilgrim.'

'So you say.'

'And I'm on a journey to heaven.'

'Well, that's very nice for you, Pippa. Pip! Pip! Hooray! and all that. But I think you're forgetting something.'

Fear slid down every bone in Pilgrim's body as she discerned the outline of the figure in the fog.

'I have nothing to say to you,' she said.

'Oh, I'm well aware of that, my dear. But do you know how rejected that makes me feel?'

'We have nothing to talk about.'

'On the contrary, we have everything to talk about! Did you really think you could forget your dear old friend Shame?'

'You're not my friend.'

'Oh, there you go again. Running away, averting your eyes, denying my very existence! How cruel you can be!'

'I want heaven.'

'Of course, Pippa, but does heaven want you?'

Terror now stirred in Pilgrim's gut.

'I believe so, yes.'

'You believe so? How reassuring. But then heaven doesn't know you, Pippa; doesn't know you at all!'

Overwhelmed by inadequacy, Pilgrim's hopes and dreams were fading fast.

'But I know you,' said Shame, 'which is why you've run so hard from me all these years. You always were a little – how shall we put it? – defective? If only people knew you as you really are, Pippa.'

Pilgrim fell to her knees and begged.

'Please go! Please!'

'Go? Go? Why would I go now?'

'Because it's time,' said a new voice.

Pilgrim looked up from the ground but saw nothing.

'Who's that?' hissed Shame.

'I'm the one you run from, Shame.'

'Grace!' said Shame, with hateful derision.

'Go in peace, Shame, but go,' said Grace. 'Your time is up.'

'My time is never up! Never!'

'You are testimony to past times not present times and you were a lie even then.'

'I will be feared!'

'Not by me, you have no substance.'

'I control Pippa!' said Shame with a loud and monstrous roar. 'Always have!'

Pilgrim was terrified.

'Shame's right, Grace,' said Pilgrim. 'If heaven truly knew who I was – '

' – they'd never let you in? That's the oldest lie in the book,' said Grace.

'I think you're losing your protégée,' said Shame.

'Really?' said Grace. 'Then step out from the mist, Shame, and show yourself. Step out so we can all see the victor in the flesh.'

'No, no!' gasped Pilgrim.

The shrouded figure breathed heavily like a lion about to pounce.

'Don't expose Shame,' pleaded Pilgrim. 'I'll turn back, Grace, but please don't expose it.'

'You're right to be fearful, Pippa,' said Shame. 'Sensible girl. Now turn back and all will be forgiven. We can return to how things were. You can bury me again!'

There was a moment of silence, a crossroads in time.

'Pilgrim.'

'Yes, Grace?'

'Stand up and walk towards Shame.'

'What?'

'Do as I say.'

'I can't.'

'You can.'

Hesitantly, Pilgrim rose from her knees.

'You don't want to be doing this,' said Shame.

'You do,' said Grace.

'I'm not sure,' said Pilgrim.

'Walk,' said Grace with perfect and persuasive confidence.

One step, two steps, three steps, Pilgrim advanced into the deep cloud towards the shape of Shame. It was like walking into hell. And then suddenly, there he was! Or rather, there it was. For this was no person but a contortion, a twisted mass of what appeared like writhing twisted string.

'Don't come so close!' hissed Shame.

'Reach out and touch,' said Grace.

Heart-pounding, Pilgrim stretched her hand towards this gaunt-eyed distortion.

'Hello, Shame,' she said.

And at the moment of greeting and touch, the creature began to combust like fat in a fire, fizzing and scalding in grotesque disintegration.

'Agghh!' screamed Pilgrim, her skin burning in a terrible pain.

But Shame was no more, the only remains a few twisted knots steaming in a viscous slime. Pilgrim stood scarred and numb. But free.

'Well done, Pilgrim.'

'That hurt.'

'The scars of battle suit you. And of course you are now free.'

'I am,' said Pilgrim.

She looked again at the door in the wall.

'It has no handle,' observed Pilgrim.

'Why would there be a handle, dear one?'

'How else can I open it?' she replied, not beyond stating the obvious, even in the Cloud of Unknowing. 'Handles are traditional.'

'But in this instance, unnecessary. We do not find heaven, Pilgrim; heaven finds us.'

'Oh I see. So I cannot break into heaven?'

'No, heaven must break into you.'

'And can heaven break into a soul so wounded?'

'A wounded soul is the gateway to heaven, sweet one. And that's where you stand now.'

In that moment, the door leapt into life, swinging wide open with a crash and a bang and a symphony of wonderful sound. Light poured out with eye-deafening force and Pilgrim was drawn inside as if by strong winds, though whether they pushed or pulled she couldn't be sure. And as she lay on the celestial ground inside, she sensed the light, heard the soaring trumpet of homecoming – but most of all? Most of all she knew peace, a rich and rounded peace quite beyond telling, a coming home to her soul and the world.

Heaven.

The twentieth stage

Her first task in the eternal city, after checking the fridge, was to answer the doorbell. It was the milkman, though not her regular one. Here was a man whose skin was black as night with a body which seemed trapped by his uniform.

'Welcome home, Pilgrim,' he said, with a smile.

'Thank you!' she replied with unreasonable happiness given that he'd only delivered a pint of milk and some bread. But then she was happy.

It was only on closing the door and returning inside that she recognised him. Word Shy! How had she been so slow? She ran back to the door, throwing it open and looking down the street. There was no one there. And she remembered the seven words. Could it really be that with those three words of greeting, his seven words were spent? Thankfulness and sadness both passed through her but did not stay, for that was his journey and not hers.

'*Happily separate, gladly relating*,' noted Pilgrim in her diary.

But just as she settled on her sofa a familiar cry called her back into the garden.

'Hello, Pippa!'

It was Consultant trimming his hedge, though to Pilgrim's ears he sounded strange, enfeebled, like a weak whistle in the wind.

'So the traveller returns,' he said, as she stepped onto the lawn. 'Tale between your legs, eh?'

'Not really, Con.'

'I tried to tell you but would you listen?'

'I'm very well, Con.'

He smiled knowingly.

'So answer me this, Pippa: if everything's so hunky dory, why come back?'

'Somehow it doesn't feel like "back".

'Same old, same old, in my book.'

'You don't understand, do you? The path I followed was not to take me from one place to another, but from here to a deeper here; from where I am to a deeper where I am.'

'Pippa's Progress, eh?'

'Perhaps "a pilgrim's journey to heaven" is better.'

'Heaven?'

Con started choking. Pilgrim, who couldn't deny her fondness for the man, moved quickly to help, surprising herself by leaping the fence. She then realised how Consultant had changed since she last saw him. Here was a haggard man, withered and dry like an Egyptian mummy.

'Are you all right, Con?' she asked.

'Something went down the wrong way.'

'A bit of heaven perhaps,' said Pilgrim. 'It can stick in people's throats.'

She led him over to a bench and sat down next to him.

'You should have come on the conference,' he said, recovering.

'Are you sure you're all right?'

'Four PowerPoint presentations and some serious blue sky thinking.'

And then Pilgrim started laughing. She couldn't help it.

'I wouldn't laugh too loud,' he said, taking umbrage.

'Why not?'

'A few things have changed round here while you've been away.'

'Like?'

'Well, for starters, you've got a real clown for a new neighbour.'

'You find him odd?'

'No, I mean he's a real clown.'

An astonished thought suddenly passed through Pilgrim's mind.

'Could you be Happy?' she asked, incredulously.

Consultant imagined she was speaking to him.

'No, I don't think so. The word's a linguistic nonsense. I'm a facilitator, an enabler – '

'No, I don't mean you, Con. I mean the clown next door. Is that his name? Is he called Mr Happy?'

Now it was Consultant's turn to be astonished.

'How could you possibly have known that?'

Pilgrim smiled.

'I trusted the path, my friend. You travel alone but meet friends along the way.'

Con looked puzzled but he was about to become more so.

The eagle in the sky had been circling for a while. But suddenly he's descending at speed, arrowing down towards Con and Pilgrim. Con takes evasive action, throwing himself behind his garden shed, but Pilgrim feels no fear. And suddenly in a flapping fury of wing and feather, the magnificent creature is next to her, perched on the bird table as a shocked sparrow hastily leaves.

'Don't worry!' says a terrified Con. 'I'll get help!'

'You need it,' says Pilgrim, as she's enfolded in the warm wings of this great soul and held neck against neck, life against life, heart against beating heart.

And miraculously, Pilgrim allows it all. She remembers the child's words by the fire: 'You must never again fear love.' She now understands. The fear of love is spent and joy races through her veins. She looks up into Jesse's warm and comprehending eyes.

'But what of my history?' she asks.

'We shall make history young again, Pilgrim.'

'Can that really be?'

'Do not be afraid – be at peace,' he says.

'And no shame?'

'Why listen to a lie?'

'Habit, I suppose.'

'Some habits are for leaving behind; there's so much we have no need of. And in time, I will return to take you with me so that where I am you shall be too.'

'And where will you be?' asks Pilgrim.

'Where there is no more crying or sorrow, for the maker and holder of heaven will wipe every tear from your eyes.'

'Heaven sounds great!'

'You are heaven, Pilgrim, and every step a kiss.'

As quickly as he came he was gone, soaring upwards, climbing into the sky and watched all the way by Pilgrim. And this was the thing: it was hard to be sure but it seemed as though the skies opened to receive him, like fabric ripped, a hole torn, before closing again with Jesse gone from her sight.

Pilgrim stood still, gazing upwards. Only slowly did she become conscious of something warm, strange and newly placed around her neck. She looked down in both fear and delight and there it was: the golden chain and pendant proclaiming her

Last seen and held in very different times, Pilgrim's legs wobbled a little. She traversed her garden fence, more slowly this time, and in a daze staggered inside. There she sat down, breathed deeply and held the pendant, feeling it press hard against her skin.

'Beloved of the earth,' she said to herself.

After a while, she looked up. There on the wall was her portrait, last seen floating in the sea. Like the rest of her furniture, it was returned to its proper place. All was quite as it had been; only entirely different. For if the canvas was returned, the image was not. The old portrait was gone, lost in the Sea of Identity, and now a blank canvas hung in its place.

'*And that's how it shall stay*,' wrote Pilgrim in her well-worn and much-travelled diary. '*I shall live the blank canvas, remain a daily adventure. How can Pippa be otherwise? How can heaven be otherwise? And for Pilgrim, every step a kiss.*'